# THE ART OF
# CHANNELING

## About the Author

Jenny Tyson (Nova Scotia, Canada) is an illustrator and writer, and practices and studies intuitive skills. She is married to Donald Tyson and enjoys working with different creative mediums.

## To Write to the Author

If you wish to contact the author or would like more information about this book, please write to the author in care of Llewellyn Worldwide Ltd. and we will forward your request. Both the author and the publisher appreciate hearing from you and learning of your enjoyment of this book and how it has helped you. Llewellyn Worldwide Ltd. cannot guarantee that every letter written to the author can be answered, but all will be forwarded. Please write to:

Jenny Tyson
℅ Llewellyn Worldwide
2143 Wooddale Drive
Woodbury, MN 55125-2989
Please enclose a self-addressed stamped envelope for reply,
or $1.00 to cover costs. If outside the U.S.A., enclose
an international postal reply coupon.

Many of Llewellyn's authors have websites with additional
information and resources. For more information,
please visit our website at http://www.llewellyn.com

# THE ART OF
# CHANNELING

## MODERN METHODS
## FOR TRUE
## *Telepathic & Spirit*
## *Communication*

# JENNY TYSON

Llewellyn Publications • Woodbury, Minnesota

FIRST EDITION
First Printing, 2022

Book design by Christine Ha
Cover design by Shira Atakpu
Interior illustration (page 93) by the Llewellyn Art Department
Interior illustrations (pages 131, 134, 137, 139, 145, 146, 147, 149, 150, 151, 152, 155, 156, 157, 159, and 161) by Jenny Tyson
Interior photos (pages 155 and 158) provided by Donald Tyson

Llewellyn Publications is a registered trademark of Llewellyn Worldwide Ltd.

**Library of Congress Cataloging-in-Publication Data (Pending)**
ISBN: 978-0-7387-7147-2

Llewellyn Worldwide Ltd. does not participate in, endorse, or have any authority or responsibility concerning private business transactions between our authors and the public.

All mail addressed to the author is forwarded but the publisher cannot, unless specifically instructed by the author, give out an address or phone number.

Any internet references contained in this work are current at publication time, but the publisher cannot guarantee that a specific location will continue to be maintained. Please refer to the publisher's website for links to authors' websites and other sources.

Llewellyn Publications
A Division of Llewellyn Worldwide Ltd.
2143 Wooddale Drive
Woodbury, MN 55125-2989
www.llewellyn.com

Printed in the United States of America

## Other Books by Jenny Tyson

*The Art of Scrying and Dowsing:*
*Foolproof Methods for ESP and Remote Viewing*
(Llewellyn, 2021)

*Spiritual Alchemy:*
*Scrying, Spirit Communication, and Alchemical Wisdom*
(Llewellyn, 2016)

# Contents

# FOREWORD

Most books on channeling, as it is now called, or mediumship, as it was called in the past, focus on the experience of spirit communication for its own sake—on how to achieve it, what it involves, and what may be expected from it. This book takes a different approach to channeling, one that may well be unique. It is concerned not with the experience of channeling itself, but with what you can gain that is of practical value by communicating with discarnate intelligences of various types. The primary objective of this new and original channeling method is to obtain factual and accurate answers to questions.

As the great spirit medium Emanuel Swedenborg observed in the eighteenth century, the problem with communicating with spirits is that they don't always tell the truth. Many channelers have been misled into delusions by the untruths that are often the fruit of conventional channeling. They have destroyed their reputations and their lives by persisting to trust the words they received, or believed themselves to have received, from spirits. This has caused skeptics to dismiss all spirit communications as fantasies and nonsense.

In this groundbreaking book, the writer asserts that it is not spirits who lie and deceive the channelers, but rather it is the channelers who deceive themselves by mistaking the expectations and beliefs of their own minds for spirit communications. Jenny Tyson contends that spirits do not lie; more than that, she maintains that spirits cannot lie, since they are part of the great Nexus that connects us all with universal mind. By using a structured method of question and response, which she devised after more than a decade of research and practical channeling experience, it is possible for a channeler to short-circuit the fantasies and expectations of the analytical mind and attain accurate communications from spirits concerning all topics, past, present, and future.

Once the self-deception of the channeler's own mental process is stilled, the spirit is able to answer any query, because the Nexus of which it is a part encompasses all time and space. This is so not only for the spirits of the dead, and for recognized categories of spiritual beings such as angels, fairies, gods and elementals, but also for extraterrestrial beings in other worlds, both those who are still living and those who have passed on to a spiritual existence. It is even true for incarnate spirits who share this planet with us, such as the spirits of other living human beings or living animals.

This unique system of channeling in some ways resembles a form of scrying, and this is not an accident. It is an outgrowth of the writer's original scrying method, which she set forth in her book *The Art of Scrying and Dowsing*. She realized that she could apply to channeling the basic method she had developed to circumvent self-deception when scrying. The same problem faces the seer in both scrying and channeling: the tendency of the active analytical mind to drown out communications from the deeper mind, which is linked to the Nexus. Under ordinary conditions, the biases of the conscious mind will always overpower and take the place of actual data arising from the deeper mind. Throughout history this has been the dilemma faced by psychics and seers.

During the course of her own scrying and channeling work, the writer came to recognize this problem, and devised a way to circumvent it. The analytical mind can never be defeated by brute force. It is always stronger and louder than the deeper mind. But its deceptive voice can be quieted to a whisper by denying it expectations and beliefs to feed upon. This is true in scrying, and equally so in channeling, which is very similar to scrying in its underlying process. In scrying, the mind of the scryer ranges through the Nexus on its own, seeking information, and in channeling it has the help of an intelligent spirit, which can seek out information independently and retrieve it.

The present book is a companion to the *Art of Scrying and Dowsing*. Great benefit will be derived from a study of both these seminal works since they complement each other. However, the *Art of Channeling* has been written to stand alone, so that nothing else is needed to acquire a full understanding of this groundbreaking new channeling method. You do not have to read the *Art of Scrying and Dowsing* to learn this new way of channeling.

Every century or so, a book comes along that is so original, so lucid, and of such great practical value that it revolutionizes its field of study. In my opinion, the *Art of Channeling* is such a book. After reading it you will understand why channeling has been such a hit-or-miss affair throughout its long and colorful history, and why even the greatest of spirit mediums in the past, such as Swedenborg, Nostradamus, Edward Kelley, and Edgar Cayce, have made inaccurate predictions. But more important than this, you will understand how they failed, and how you can overcome the obstacles that caused their failures. With this book, channeling for the first time becomes a true science. I have no hesitation in calling it a landmark text in the field of spirit communication.

*—Donald Tyson*
Cape Breton, Nova Scotia

# CHAPTER ONE
# CHANNELING OVERVIEW

Channeling is a way of using intuition to discern communications from the universe of spirits, which is called the Nexus. This universe is usually invisible and inaudible to those who live in the physical universe. Humans and other physical creatures inhabit both the Nexus and the physical universe. Our focus and attention, however, are centered primarily on the physical universe, and effort has to be made to focus our attention on perceptions coming from the Nexus.

Perceptions are what we sense with both our physical and our nonphysical senses. These include hearing, sight, smell, taste, and touch. Some say we also have a nonphysical sixth sense that is focused mainly on the Nexus. I believe the physical senses are based on this so-called sixth sense, rather than the nonphysical sense being a separate perceptive ability. In my opinion, the physical world springs from the Nexus as a manifestation and solidification of certain properties of that universe.

As spiritual and physical beings, we have access to both the Nexus and the physical universe. Because of this inseparable connection, learning to channel, scry, or do magick is only a matter of understanding how we perceive the relationship between the physical universe and the Nexus, and applying that understanding to our purposes. In the case of this book, the purpose is to learn to channel. Do not be worried about whether or not you have the ability to channel. The method I present here is very easy to use. Everyone who has tried the techniques that are laid out in both this book and my earlier book *The Art of Scrying and Dowsing* (Llewellyn, 2021) has been able to channel and scry within the first few tries. This includes a few skeptics who were rather shocked at the results. The primary requirement to learn these techniques is reading and following directions. This system is not belief-based. If you have doubts as to the existence of channeling, spirits, or anything else discussed in this book, I encourage you to apply its techniques in a practical way to address your questions.

Channeling is a way of creating a bridge so that communication can occur between the living souls of the Nexus, whom we do not normally see or hear, and those of us who inhabit the physical universe. As spiritual beings, we can deliberately initiate interaction with the Nexus through the use of our thoughts, mental focus, and emotions. All humans and even some of the more complex animals, including mammals and reptiles, have been observed to use this interactive ability.

Channeling also includes telepathy between physical beings living in the physical universe. I add telepathy to the definition of channeling because telepathic perception between physical beings is subjectively identical to channeling intelligences who live primarily in non-three-dimensional realities. It is spirit-to-spirit communication, regardless of whether or not the spirits inhabit a physical body.

## Understanding the Nexus

The Latin root for the word Nexus simply means "to bind, connect." Think of the Nexus as a crossroads between the physical and nonphysical universes. By traversing this crossroads using certain techniques that can be learned, you will be able to perceive information that is normally invisible and inaudible. The information available in the Nexus is accessible to all conscious, self-aware beings.

In this book I provide a safe and tested structure by which you can efficiently access your inherent ability to interact with other spirits and perceive information sent from them. It is designed to help you, as a channeler, focus your mind and create a reliable thread of communication through the underlying abstract universal consciousness, linking you with unique spiritual entities and physical entities capable of telepathic communication. When you channel, you communicate with spirits and interact with the universal awareness that includes all life and consciousness.

There are no inherent limitations to channeling. If a particular entity cannot answer your inquiry, another will step in, or you will find yourself directly and seamlessly accessing universal consciousness. This universal awareness appears to be some kind of Nexus-based, map-like structure that is an interactive compendium or recording of the doings of all life and all time. It includes beings, events, appearances, and activities, among other things. All knowledge, even that which is beyond the technological development of the earth, is present in that Nexus-based, conscious, living, and interactive map.

Using the method in this book, you will not be differentiating between individual spirits and the Nexus structure, because it is almost impossible to tell the difference between them when you are in a channeling session. Data obtained by channeling is the same regardless of whether you interact with a spirit, a living being, or universal consciousness. I refer to the entities you will interact with as spirits, contacts, or spirit contacts. These terms are interchangeable and represent individual spirits, telepathic contacts, and interactive Nexus structures.

In this chapter I would like to outline the major aspects and general procedure of channeling. The basic session method is similar to that used for scrying but is modified to adapt to the unique needs of channeling. The first book published on this method was *The Art of Scrying and Dowsing*. Even those who have not read the scrying book should have little trouble learning how to channel. The information presented here can be used by itself for channeling, or it can be applied as a supplement to the scrying method that I described in my earlier book. It does not matter which of these two books you read first.

Let's look at some of the characteristics of the channeling method I use.

## Exclusion

There are a few unique aspects to my channeling technique. One of these is the practice of hiding information from the channeler's conscious mind. This practice is called *hiding the target* or *hiding the inquiry*. If you are interested in channeling, you probably have questions you want to ask spirit contacts. These questions, or inquiries, that the channeler wishes to put to the contact have to be hidden, and the session done without the channeler's conscious knowledge of what the questions are while the channeling is being done. That's right—the channeler does not know the question being asked of the entity or spirit while they are in a channeling session. This practice is also known as *exclusion*, because it excludes the information-processing and categorizing aspects of the channeler's conscious mind. It is this information-processing mechanism that causes trouble with accuracy when channeling.

## Focus

This leads us to the second characteristic of channeling sessions that I wish to discuss, and that is focus. The channeling session must always have a very specific focus. I never teach channeling or any other intuitive skill in such a way that a door is opened and communication is received in a random or unstructured way. The session will always have a specific spirit and specific questions being asked of that spirit. This is done to ensure high-quality and accurate channeling. Having a specific focus and hiding the inquiry may seem contradictory at first glance, but as you progress through the material presented in this book, you will see that these practices are beneficial to the integrity of the channeled information.

## Bias

Why are these two practices of hiding the inquiry and having a specific focus taught in this book? Because they help to inhibit what I call *belief bias* and *expectation bias*. These biases are the most detrimental obstacles to accurate channeling.

Belief bias occurs when you have both conscious and subconscious assumptions about the spirit or the information the spirit is asked to channel. Expectation bias happens when you expect that certain things will be communicated by a particular spirit. These biases cause the channeler to anticipate that a certain answer will be given based on the nature of the question being asked and the identity of the spirit giving the response. These assumptions and beliefs are so powerful that they can overwhelm the responses of the spirit with whom the channeler has established communication. The result of belief and expectation biases is inaccurate channeled responses that appear to come from the spirit contact. These two biases are the source of the most common causes of channeling errors, such as failed predictions, false or inaccurate information, and information that gives the appearance that the spirit is being deceitful.

When inaccurate information is channeled, the result is a loss of trust in the abilities of the channeler and disbelief in the reality of the entity being channeled, both by the channeler and by anyone else who may be aware of the channeling. But this is not the fault of the channeler or the entity; it is due to belief and expectation biases, which subconsciously tell the channeler what they want to hear, or think they should hear, instead of allowing accurate information to be perceived.

Emanuel Swedenborg, the famous Swedish channeler of the eighteenth century, once made the observation that spirits are not to be trusted because they tend to lie. He wrote in his *Spiritual Diary*:

> When spirits begin to speak with man, he must beware lest he believe them in anything; for they say almost anything; things are fabricated by them, and they lie; for if they were permitted to relate what heaven is, and how things are in the heavens, they would tell so many lies, and indeed with solemn affirmation, that man would be astonished; wherefore, when spirits were speaking, I was not permitted to have faith in the things which they related.—1748, March 20. For they are extremely fond of fabricating: and whenever any subject of discourse is proposed, they think that they know it, and give their opinions one after another, one in one way, and another in another, altogether as if they knew; and if man then listens and believes, they press on, and deceive, and seduce in divers ways.[1]

Swedenborg's understanding of channeling inaccuracy was a bit simplistic. It is not so much that spirits lie as it is that their communications are overpowered by the beliefs and expectations in the mind of the channeler—beliefs and

---

1. Emanuel Swedenborg, *The Spiritual Diary of Emanuel Swedenborg*, trans. George Bush, vol. 2 of 5 (London: James Speirs, 1883), 19, entry 1622.

expectations that the channeler may not even be aware of having. These biases shape the perceptions the channeler has of the channeled spirit's responses, and the result is false information.

The best way to reduce belief and expectation biases is for the channeler to conceal the questions that are to be put to the spirit. They must be concealed not from the spirit but from the channeler. In addition to concealment, the questions selected for the channeling session must be well focused, with very specific goals. These requirements pose a challenge. How are we to ask questions of a spirit when the question itself must be hidden from the conscious knowledge of the channeler? The solution to this dilemma is to use what I call the grab bag technique. This is another feature of my channeling system.

## Grab Bag Technique

To use the grab bag technique, multiple questions are written down for the spirit contact in a specialized format that creates the right conditions for accurate channeling. At least four of these formatted questions are placed in the grab bag for the channeling session. The container for the questions is a small cloth bag. The slips of paper must be identical in appearance and folded in the same manner, so the channeler cannot tell one from another. The questions are composed using a word structure that creates a very specific and narrow focus. Regardless of which question is selected from the bag by the channeler, it will meet the requirements of being focused and specific. The information obtained during the channeling session will reflect these very specific, formatted inquiries, even though the channeler does not consciously know what they are at the time of the session.

At the start of the channeling session, a single slip of paper bearing one of the questions is taken out of the grab bag and set aside without being unfolded or examined. In this way, it is possible to select a properly formatted question but still not know the question. Both the channeler's deeper mind and the spirit being channeled know what it is, because the deeper mind and universal consciousness have access to all the information existing in all possible universes from all times, past, present, and future. The conscious mind of the channeler, where beliefs and expectations are centered, does not have access to the goal of the session. That lack of information makes it impossible for the conscious mind to anticipate a response. Because of this exclusion, belief and expectation biases are reduced. The subtle, accurate, and true communications from the channeled entity may be perceived and recorded. The process of hiding the subject of inquiry isolates the part of the mind that creates accuracy problems when channeling and allows the information from the deeper mind to surface.

## The Cuckoo Dilemma

I have laid out for you the basic challenge with channeling—why the information received from spirits is so often incorrect and how to overcome it. It is not that spirits lie, as Swedenborg asserted, but rather that the expectation bias of the channeler distorts and taints the information given by spirits. Expectations, both conscious and unconscious, overwhelm the spirit communication and displace it in the same way a cuckoo chick pecks the chick of another bird species to death in its nest.

A cuckoo hen will lay an egg in the nest of a compatible songbird. When the cuckoo chick hatches, it kills the offspring of the songbird. The mother songbird thinks the cuckoo is its own chick and begins to feed it. In this same manner, channelers tend to feed their own belief and expectation biases, which distort or wholly destroy the results of their channeling sessions. In a metaphorical sense, these biases "kill" the information arising from the deeper mind and take its place. When the questions asked of the spirit are hidden from the channeler, the harmful effects of these inherent biases are significantly reduced.

Now that you understand the problem of belief and expectation biases, you understand why I created this method and what problems I was trying to address. This system was developed through experimentation and study over the past ten years. In my first book, *Spiritual Alchemy* (Llewellyn, 2016), you can see where I started with this channeling technique. I was very focused on the experience of spirit communication. As I developed greater skill in channeling, my focus changed to achieving accuracy in channeled communications. Finally, after I had learned how accuracy could be attained, I sought to develop techniques that are efficient, reliable, and easy to learn. The system described in the book you are reading is the result of those years of development and practice.

Let me continue with a description of the framework of a channeling session so that you will be able to orient yourself and not become lost when I move on to the discussion of specific details.

## Session Structure

A vital feature of my channeling system is session structure. I devised a formal outline for the channeler to use during a session. The channeler fills in various pieces of the outline. This somewhat mechanical structure allows the session to be very low-key, with minimal emotional involvement. It enhances both consistency and accuracy. The session structure makes it easier for the channeler to carefully analyze the channeled material after the session is concluded, which in turn helps the channeler cover topics more thoroughly and also discover new topics of interest.

## Communication Techniques

I describe several communication techniques in this book. The backbone of my channeling technique is automatic writing and sketching. The emphasis is on sketching. When documenting any intuitive perception, sketching always takes priority over written information. When the channeled material is reality-checked later on during the feedback session, sketching almost always proves to be one of the most consistently accurate parts of the session. It does not require the channeler to be an artist. The sketches are quickly drawn, so that even an experienced artist will be working mostly with stick figures and primitive outlines.

There are two secondary communication techniques presented in this book in addition to automatic writing and sketching. The first is dowsing and the second is trance channeling.

## Dot Matrix and Spirit Board Dowsing

I went over dowsing in considerable detail in my earlier book *The Art of Scrying and Dowsing*. The dowsing methods I present in *The Art of Channeling* do not require special tools or talent. The first method, dot matrix dowsing, is a good beginner technique and can be done with no more than a pencil and some paper. It is used to clarify channeled information by eliciting "yes" or "no" answers to simple questions. The other dowsing method involves the use of a pendulum.

Pendulum dowsing is a useful skill to acquire. It does not demand any particular talent, although it does require a bit of practice and good observational skills. The type of pendulum I recommend for pendulum dowsing is a darning needle, which is a blunt sewing needle around two inches in length that is used for yarn and knitting. If you wish to purchase a pendulum for dowsing, I suggest going with a very lightweight needle-size metal or wooden pendulum and attaching fine sewing thread to it.

The pendulum is used in conjunction with a spirit board, which is a large, flat surface of wood, cloth, or cardboard that has the letters of the alphabet spaced evenly over its surface. Traditionally, an indicator called a *pointer* or *planchette* is used to intuitively pick out letters on the board to form words. In the technique presented here for purposes of channeling, a pendulum is used in place of a pointer. This is essentially a specialized dowsing technique. The board is employed only after automatic sketching is completed. The inquiry continues to be hidden during the spirit board session.

This technique is a bit different from the traditional Ouija board game that is more commonly used by those seeking spirit communications. The spirit board is not used for basic channeling, but rather for one-word clarifications and yes-no answers to questions. The spirit board does not allow sketching, which is the highest priority for information transmitted from the Nexus. Therefore, it is of limited utility in the system I am presenting here.

I address the response-anticipation problem with the board (which is essentially the same as expectation bias) by hiding the letters on the spirit board under a cloth. A pendulum is used to locate letters, and straight pins are thrust through the cloth to mark out the response. The channeler sees only the blank cloth that covers the board. The letters of the response are then sorted out like an anagram.

## Trance Channeling

The other secondary communication technique is trance channeling, in which a trance state is induced and communication takes place in that state. Like the spirit board, trance channeling is of limited use, particularly for a solitary practitioner, as the trance cannot be properly maintained while sketching by most people. There are those who can both write and sketch while in trance, and for such people this trance technique will enhance their already developed abilities. However, the focus of this book is primarily on those who have been falsely led to believe that they do not have talent for channeling or are just starting out with it.

Trance channeling is best done with a partner. If a partner cannot be found, then it is essential to have a digital recorder to record the channeled information. The basic trance session is done after the paper session is completed and before the inquiry is disclosed to the channeler. Though trance channeling is an advanced skill, I do recommend that everyone try to do some work with it. The unique perspective and intensity of the experience can be helpful to your overall development as a channeler. The mental control and focus you develop as you learn to do trance channeling will help you indirectly with your tabletop sessions. If you increase your focus, you will improve the overall quality of your sessions. The effect is indirect and stems from personal growth. Be aware that channeling in trance does not automatically result in more accurate information than channeling in normal waking consciousness.

The experience of trance channeling varies greatly. As with other types of channeling, the focus should always be on obtaining high-quality, accurate information. You should not compare your experiences in trance to the experiences recorded by other trance channelers. It is always best to accept your personal experience for what it is. My goal during trance channeling sessions is not the experience of trance channeling itself, but the acquisition of accurate information.

## Feedback

Feedback is another key aspect of my channeling technique that is vital for improving accuracy. After you complete your channeling session, regardless of which type of session you are doing, you will compare the information the spirit channeled to you with what is known about the topic or the spirit's life, depending on the focus of the session. You study the spirit's communication perception by perception, and compare it to the known data about the spirit's physical life or the topic you are seeking information about.

Through this process you can discover where you are channeling belief and expectation biases instead of the spirit's actual communications. It should be assumed that the spirit is channeling accurate information, because the spirit contact always has access to such information. It dwells in the Nexus, and all the knowledge and information that exists may be found there in perfect and precise detail. It should be assumed that the channeler makes the error when an error occurs. Even if the spirit intends to deceive the channeler, if the focus of the channeler is on accurate information, the deeper mind will always go to the source that provides the desired information. If the spirit does not provide it, the focus of the channeler will automatically go to the universal mind, which cannot deceive and always has the true and accurate information.

## Advanced Practices

The basic channeling sessions in this book will be done sitting at a desk or table with a pencil and paper. For the most part, I will be teaching you to work in a state of normal waking consciousness. Working in this way is accurate and will provide you with the essential channeling experience. It will also give you unlimited access to the spirits and any information you desire. The basic techniques contain everything you need.

However, there are experiences you may want to have in addition to the basic channeling session. For this reason, I have included some teaching on advanced practices. These are not essential for gaining information. Instead, they enhance your experience of channeling. The advanced practices covered in this book are front-loading, the use of settings, and group work. These techniques will be used as supplements and aids to add interest and variety, and to help you, as a channeler, maintain your focus and have fun with it.

The basic sessions, done sitting at a desk using your core skills, provide adequate contact with high-quality, accurate information. If you are a beginner, you should stick with the basic sessions until you have a good feel for the technique and are comfortable with the session structure and procedures. As you advance, you can incorporate additional techniques according to your personal interests. None of these advanced techniques are required. They do not increase accuracy, but only add interest and enhance the experience.

## Front-Loading

*Front-loading* is a remote viewing term describing information that is available to the conscious mind of the channeler (or remote viewer) prior to the channeling session. Front-loading places a significant burden on the channeler and can be very difficult to work with. The use of front-loading has to be done in a limited and structured way so that it does not create a situation where you are building a story based on belief or expectation bias.

Even as an advanced practitioner, you can develop issues with bias if you front-load your channeling sessions frequently or with too much information. Allowing yourself knowledge of the session goals not only creates problems with that session but also can cause your skills to deteriorate. This is due to the fact that your perceptions will always favor, and usually reinforce, your biases in subtle and sometimes not so subtle ways. It is easy to fall into the trap of telling people what they expect to hear or telling yourself what you believe is the response that should come from a given spirit regarding a topic. This deterioration can be insidious and difficult to detect. It can be reversed by doing repeated sessions in which you hide the inquiry, but it may take a bit of time before the effect of this exclusion results in an improvement in accuracy.

When you train for front-loading, the goal is to find a way to separate the part of your mind protected by belief and expectation biases from the information coming in from the Nexus. The biases protect your inner personal beliefs. They also protect your mind from too much information that contradicts what you perceive as reality. This is important in maintaining personal boundaries. Expectation and belief biases are survival mechanisms and are vital to the integrity of the personality.

I have observed that belief and expectation biases play a significant role in what is perceived. They can even come into play when you hide the inquiry. Belief and expectation biases are very powerful mental tendencies that protect the integrity of the mind. There are some training tools that can be used to decrease the bias issues with front-loading. The session tools that I find effective will be presented in chapter 14.

I do not recommend using trance channeling with front-loading. The intensity of belief and expectations biases becomes more powerful when trance is used.

## Use of Setting

Settings can enhance the channeling experience. Basically, the setting is how you prepare your environment for a session. Settings create an immersive experience. This is when you create a physical environment that makes you feel mystical or a séance-like environment, or you channel in another place (such as an outdoor circle) that separates you from the normal world and gives a feeling of being at the bridge between the physical world and the Nexus. Studies, including the Philip experiment described in the 1976 book *Conjuring Up Philip*, indicate that if an immersive setting is used, there is an increased likelihood of physical manifestations of a paranormal nature.[2]

Settings may include things like a space set apart for channeling, candles, photos, drawings, music, and sometimes special equipment, such as digital recorders, infrared or heat-sensing video cameras, and magnetometers. Settings are usually specific to the type of spirit contact that is being channeled. Use of a special setting does not increase the accuracy of channeled information and is mainly employed to enhance the experience of the session and increase the intensity of the sense of contact with the entity.

## Group Practice

Group practice utilizes the core session procedure. It is frequently employed in conjunction with setting and may be focused more on manifestation than on information. In this book I cover how to do an information session as a group. In the past, a special medium was used in a group, and the remainder of the group members were passive observers. My philosophy on how to run a channeling group is a bit different from the traditional approach. I believe that the group should have a facilitator but that all members of the group should do their own channeling session. The entire group can work with the same inquiry. Hidden questions and the skills of automatic writing, dowsing, and spirit communication boards are used in the session. Trance channeling and immersive settings may be added as desired.

---

2. Iris M. Owen, with Margaret Sparrow, *Conjuring Up Philip* (New York: Harper & Row, 1976).

I do not recommend group practice training for front-loaded sessions. Not everyone has the ability to do a front-loaded session accurately or comfortably. Generally a group will be made up of both beginners and advanced practitioners, and this needs to be taken into account before adding the advanced skills of trance channeling and immersive settings.

## Protection and Rituals

One of the goals of this book is to provide a method of channeling that is natural, safe, and effective but also efficient. The channeling session can be done in as little as fifteen minutes, and the learning time for the session structure is about an hour. I participate in groups (magical practice groups and human-initiated extraterrestrial contact groups) that practice channeling without any circle, candles, incense, or other protection devices or rituals. I have never seen a problem with doing channeling without these devices. I personally do not do protection rituals, and feel they tend to make my mental focus rather negative. There can be a problem with the ritual creating an immersive belief bias situation that is unpleasant. In other words, you can shoot yourself in the foot to protect yourself from an imaginary bear.

In this book I encourage the reader to focus on channeling and not worry about ritual-based protection. Work with the techniques and trust that your focus will keep anything unpleasant away from you. I have found effective ways to deal with the occasional situation where spirits engage in attention-getting behavior. If you do channeling sessions with consistent structure, good focus, and honest feedback, malicious spirits tend to leave you alone. Handling feedback properly and reality-checking the information from a channeling session seem to be the strongest deterrents against negative entity activity. These techniques and session characteristics are built into the structure of the channeling system. This system is also designed to be used with other ritual-based systems such as Wiccan circles, formal grimoires, and Spiritualist or shamanic circles. If you prefer to do protection circles, opening rituals, and dismissal rituals, then simply add the channeling session structure to the established ritual. I discuss integration of settings with the basic channeling session structure in chapter 16.

## Integrating Channeling with Scrying

When this channeling book was originally written, it was part of the intuitive techniques I had developed for *The Art of Scrying and Dowsing*. The two books were originally two parts of one book. It was necessary to split the material for reasons of manuscript length and focus. You will find that the channeling techniques in this book interface quite naturally with the scrying techniques in *The Art of Scrying and Dowsing*.

If you are doing a scrying session, you can use the same tasking and the same grab bag draw for a channeling session. I would suggest doing the channeling session immediately after the scrying session. The techniques of automatic writing and sketching that I describe later in this book are similar to the internal scrying techniques in *The Art of Scrying and Dowsing*. In combining the two techniques of scrying and channeling, you will be able to perceive detailed high-quality information. You have the potential of producing work equal to or better than the great seers of the past, such as Nostradamus and Edward Kelley. Both of these remarkable men have contemplated their strengths and weaknesses as seers from their exalted state in the afterlife and have kindly contributed techniques to this book.

I realize that not everyone who reads this book will view such things in the same way that I do. Both this book and *The Art of Scrying and Dowsing* are designed to be used by anyone, regardless of their belief, or lack of belief, in spirits. However, I have to present things as I view them. The perception of the contributions to this book by Nostradamus and Kelley is there, regardless of whether they originated in my subconscious, from wishful thinking, or through spirit communication. The quality of the material in both the scrying book and this channeling book show the innovations and advances that can be made by using the original techniques I have presented to you.

Because many of the concepts in this book are new or not traditionally associated with the art of channeling, I had to use specialized terminology to describe the unique aspects of this method of channeling. I have included the obscure and possibly confusing terms in the glossary at the end of the book.

## CHAPTER TWO
# SPIRIT SELECTION

Allan Kardec, the great nineteenth-century French authority on Spiritism, said that there are two basic forms of interaction with spirits. He wrote, "Spirit phenomena are of two kinds, physical and intelligent effects."[3] The first kind of interaction is physical manifestation, and the second is the transmission of intelligible information. In this book I focus on the transmission of information.

This chapter will help you formulate a list of spirits you wish to contact during a channeling session, and give you an idea of the information those spirits can provide. Each type of spirit listed in this chapter has the ability to answer questions about a particular set of topics with the greatest possible insight. While it is true that all spirits have access to all information via the Nexus, some types relate better to a given topic than others. For example, a canine or feline spirit would be able to tell you more about how scent plays a role in their perception of a topic. However, a canine's or feline's insight would not be as good as a human's if they were asked to describe the political climate of Europe in 1325.

Next, I will go over the various classes of spirit contacts you are likely to interact with and explain why some are better than others for obtaining different kinds of information. There are countless kinds of spirit contacts, and most of them have not yet even been identified. Discovering new classes of spirit

---

3. Allan Kardec, *Book on Mediums* (Boston, MA: Colby and Rich, 1874), 49.

contacts, as well as interacting with the individual entities described in these pages, is part of the fun of channeling. In this chapter, I give suggestions as to the kind of information that best relates to various spirit types. The different types of spirit contacts provide contrasting philosophies and perspectives for any given inquiry.

The entities described in this chapter are only recommendations of spirits you could choose to contact. Always keep in mind that spirit contacts are flexible and have instant access to the vast network of the Nexus. Their ability to retrieve information is, as far as I can tell, unlimited. The physical universe's limitations of time and space do not exist in the Nexus. This flexibility has led some to believe that spirits are, in fact, no more than a psychological phenomenon. I do not think this is the case. A spirit contact merely has easier access to Nexus information than a corporeal entity can obtain from the physical world.

The possible exceptions to this would be the servitor, egregore, and homunculus. These types of spirits are human-made and appear to have more restricted abilities due to the limitations of their makers at the time of their creation. They are designed—or, in the case of egregores, sometimes arise spontaneously—with a particular purpose to perform specific functions. They also have a limited span of existence. The longer they are permitted by their makers to exist, the more self-aware and capable they become.

## Human Spirits

The first type of spirit, that of a human being, will have a verifiable past history. Some of these spirits are historical figures whose lives are well documented. Their histories can be used to check channeling for accuracy and focus. The details of the physical lives, beliefs, and activities of human spirits provide rich session feedback, which is important when developing channeling skills. Spirits of earthly human beings are the best spirit contacts for beginners to work with, because the channeler can relate to them more easily than to a spirit with a nonhuman origin.

## Extraterrestrial Intelligences

This second type of spirit contact I will call extraterrestrial intelligences. This term covers both physical and nonphysical entities. These can be living entities who dwell physically on an exoplanet (a planet that lies beyond our solar system) or who exist in a nonphysical state much like that of a human spirit. Some have the ability to focus their consciousness and personality into an astral form that is a spirit double of their physical being. There are some extraterrestrial species who use telepathy as their primary form of interpersonal communication. These are primary telepathic entities. These can include species whose planets are no longer in existence, having died or been killed. (Planets are mortal, just like all other physical beings.) The variety of this group is beyond counting and the number of entities beyond comprehension.

It is possible for channelers to misidentify a Nexus-based extraterrestrial entity as an angel or a nature spirit. For example, the Enochian calls and keys recorded in the magical diaries of the Elizabethan sage Dr. John Dee (1527–1609) have achieved enormous stature in modern Western magic as powerful invocations. They were assumed by Dr. Dee to be written in the language of the angels of heaven, but I believe they offer a glimpse of a nonhuman language from a civilization on another planet—a civilization that may still be in existence. Dr. Dee assumed that angels were all one species and that they used language in the same way a human being would. It was this assumption that may have led to the misidentification.

The word *angel* means messenger, and angels were not always considered to be supernatural. I am led to believe that most biblical angels could be human beings from the future, or living people (mystics, mediums, and psychics) who have simply performed the function of messenger via intuition or spiritual channeling. Biblical angels who were nonhuman, supernatural beings were recorded in a couple of visions, particularly those described in the biblical book of Revelation and book of Ezekiel. These can be more logically interpreted as extraterrestrials.

When I reexamined the Enochian visions using the techniques I talk about both in this book and in *The Art of Scrying and Dowsing*, I found strong indications that the language belonged to a humanoid species of extraterrestrials physically living on an exoplanet of unknown origin. The focus of Edward Kelley when talking to the angels was on heaven or the sky. Because of this, and the other data he perceived, I think the easiest and most reasonable interpretation is that Enochian is a nonhuman, extraterrestrial language. The categories of spirits presented in this chapter do not have rigid boundaries, so an entity such as an angel or extraterrestrial may fit into more than one of them.

## Religion-Based Entities

The religious-based entities can be spirit entities that do not take on a physical body at all and dwell completely in their native spirit universe, or entities that can take on the appearance of a physical form and interact with the physical universe when they wish to. They can be saints (of any religion), angels, demons, djinn, fairies, elementals, or deities. These types of entities have a complex mythology, usually associated with a particular religion. They may be worshiped as divine, feared as diabolical, or linked with miracles and supernatural manifestations. As I said concerning extraterrestrial entities, a particular type of being may fit into more than one category of spirit.

There is usually a substantial body of literature that prescribes how interaction with these types of entities should be done and details some of their characteristics. Though we have a rich fund of lore on these entities to draw from, we actually do not know much about them. In Western occult practice, a mythological entity is called up for a very narrow and specific purpose, such as fulfilling a task for the channeler. Manifestation rather than information is often the top priority with this style of interaction. However, even though these entities are usually petitioned for favors, they do have access to knowledge that may provide a channeler with interesting and informative sessions.

## Spirit Animals

Animal spirits may be living or they may be Nexus-based entities. They can communicate, although their communications often have a strange feel to them, and they offer unusual perspectives, particularly where sensory experiences are concerned. An example of this would be a wolf spirit, who will describe its world in terms of scent. This is a sense that is very poorly developed in human beings. Learning about the world in terms of scent is a unique experience for a channeler, who cannot physically do what a wolf or dog can do with its sense of smell.

Living animals can communicate by means of telepathy, but it is on a subconscious level. The physical animal may sense something but will not be consciously aware of what is happening. Animal spirits do not communicate with verbal language. This is where sketching your impressions during a channeling session becomes particularly useful. Any language-based perception from an animal spirit is due to mental processing coupled with belief and expectation biases. If you find this happening in session, trace the verbal communication to a deeper level and the perception should be a bit more accurate.

## Nature Spirits

Nature spirits are a generic category that describes spirits loosely associated with the earth or various features of the earth. Channeling nature spirits is an essential aspect of shamanism and similar practices. Nature spirits are usually discovered by the channeler. By this I mean that the channeler goes into an area of interest in the forest, or another wild place, and tries to make contact with a spirit associated with that area.

My first discovery of a nature spirit was a creek on a hiking trail near my home. I was using a voice recorder and I inquired at the creek if there were any spirits who were willing to talk into the recorder for me. When I played the recording later in the hike, I realized that I had picked up the voice of a spirit. I returned to the creek and was able to obtain additional recordings.

Ideally, sessions with nature spirits should be done at their associated locations or with their associated elements, such as a body of water. The Nexus will provide information if the spirit cannot respond, but you will have a better experience if you work with the associated location of the spirit you are channeling.

## Servitors, Egregores, and Homunculi

The final category concerns spirits generated by intelligent thought and force of will. These are usually related to occult work. Common types of these spirits are egregores, servitors, and homunculi. Egregores are spirits of group consciousness—the spirits of political movements, social organizations, religious cults, and so on. They may be deliberately created by a group, or they may arise spontaneously from a shared group purpose. Servitors are spirits deliberately created by magicians for specific tasks, such as protection or finding treasure. Homunculi are materialized servitors in the form of little human beings. They are associated with alchemy and are created by an alchemical process. These types of spirits are helpful entities for finding information and moving energies for manifestation. They are of limited intelligence and are employed for very specific purposes. They do not have the flexibility to do anything outside of the narrow parameters of their creation and domain.

## Telepathic Contact with Living Beings

Living humans and other living beings can also be contacted using channeling. When this happens, it is called *telepathy*. With most humans, telepathy occurs on a subconscious, or deeper mind, level. The information is usually subtle, based on images and emotions. You may not even be aware that you are doing it. For instance, telepathy comes into play when you assess whether or not someone is safe to be with. The sense of safety or danger you feel is a result of telepathic contact. This intuitive sense is how telepathy feels when it occurs naturally. It is an everyday occurrence with all human beings. Animals such as cats, dogs, and horses also use this intuitive interaction.

Telepathy can be established with any living physical entity, including creatures such as domestic or wild animals. It can be also used with extraterrestrial intelligences. The difference between channeling a spirit and telepathy is that when engaging in telepathy with humans and lower animals, generally there is no conscious awareness by the other party that the channeler is communicating with them. They may have a sense of being watched or a feeling that something odd is going on, but it is usually undetectable on a conscious level. Such feelings are generally disregarded by modern humans, who have drifted out of touch with their intuition.

Extraterrestrial intelligences vary in their ability to use telepathy. I am not certain as to which ones are consciously aware of the communication attempt. A few species are primary telepaths, but their communication techniques and emotional makeup are not natural to a human, so we experience substantial challenges in understanding them. How we work with the channeling session structure has to be altered somewhat to accurately comprehend what they are communicating. The evidence I have is that most extraterrestrial primary telepaths are not consciously aware of human-initiated telepathy unless certain conditions exist. I believe those conditions are a matter of focus on the part of both the extraterrestrial intelligence and the channeler.

Humans do not possess a great deal of development in telepathic skills when compared to more advanced species who have focused on mental and intuitive development for many generations. One way of dealing with this deficit is to increase the number of trained human channelers and have them work in small groups in unison, applying the same technique at exactly the same time. If done with good unity, this will improve the strength of the signal line, possibly raising it to the point where the extraterrestrial will be aware of the contact attempt. Even if this being cannot perceive the channeler at a conscious level, accurate information from the deeper mind and Nexus can be perceived by the channeler.

In times past, people studied and trained to detect telepathic messages. A number of examples of this are described in *Steganographia*, a fifteenth-century magical text by the German abbot Johannes Trithemius (1462–1516). In *Steganographia* he describes the use of messenger spirits, and some of the results of his experiments with them.[4] The experiments included telepathic contact with other abbots and monasteries. Most of his work with the spirits involved espionage for the local ruler. Based on the information in *Steganographia*, it may be surmised that there were a number of monasteries that had trained abbots with whom Trithemius communicated using telepathy and spirit-contact intermediaries.

With the advancement of electronic communications, telepathy has been left by the wayside for the most part. This skill is dismissed by most people as fantasy or delusion. However, this attitude only indicates a sad lack of knowledge of how telepathy and channeling actually work. We have devolved from the greater mental and spiritual abilities possessed by our ancestors. This needs to be reversed if we are to survive in the long term.

The content of the information telepathically received usually does not give an indication of whether or not the entity being channeled, either in the spirit or the body, is aware of the process on a conscious level. If you meet someone you have contacted in this way, it will likely create in them a vague feeling of déjà vu. It is difficult to know if you are being contacted telepathically. If you

---

4. I am aware of the modern view that *Steganographia* is nothing but a code book of ciphers disguised as a spirit grimoire, but based on my experimentation with it, this is not my conclusion.

do become aware of it, usually it is not an intense experience but rather a subtle sense of being watched. Sometimes, especially with extraterrestrial entities, ringing or other sounds in the ears that do not have an external source are heard by the channeler.

The more intense emotional contact experiences may be a result of your own shadow and thoughtforms. These experiences can be mistaken for telepathic contact attempts. They are aspects of your spiritual personality that can take on a form that appears to be separate from you. Servitors are an example of the same type of apparition, but are intentionally created, personal thoughtforms. Shadows are the same sort of entity but are created unintentionally. The communication experience can be emotionally intense, and it can sometimes cause supernatural phenomena to physically manifest.

A validation process I describe in chapter 13, which is on spontaneous channeling, will enable you to determine whether or not a particular experience is from telepathic contact or is the result of a personal thoughtform giving the appearance of a contact experience. You always experience your own spiritual aspects with far greater intensity than you do something coming from an intelligence that is distinct from you.

Even when using techniques such as those described in *Steganographia*, you can make mistakes in perception. These errors occur in scrying, channeling, and other interactive experiences for the same reasons. Belief and expectation biases will superimpose and overwhelm the channel in telepathy in exactly the same way they do during channeling and scrying. From the perspective of the channeler, there is no perceivable difference between channeling and telepathy, and no viable, dependable way, while you are in a channeling session, to determine whether or not you are channeling a living, physical being or a spirit inhabiting the Nexus or the interactive aspects of the Nexus itself.

Both telepathy and channeling are unlimited by time and space. You can go forward into the future, backward into the past, and in any direction in the present and (as far as I know) in any universe. The procedure for contacting spirits or using telepathy to communicate with living beings is the same. I have found that the best way to tell what you are channeling is through the validation (or feedback) session. This specialized session, which is done after channeling has been completed, can shed light on the nature of the experience. Controlled session structure and hidden inquiries, along with validation sessions, will help you verify or refute any spontaneous contact. It is the best way I have found to ascertain the validity of perceived information coming from outside a formal channeling session.

## Selection of Spirit Contacts

The entity you select for channeling should be one in whom you have only a mild interest. Strong emotional attachment is detrimental to accurate channeling. It does not matter if the emotional attachment is positive or negative. Anxiety, intense love, desperation, grief, anger, lust, and fear are all emotions destructive to the integrity of your session, particularly for a beginner. Mild curiosity and calmness, friendliness without being emotionally needy or clingy, and a balanced awareness are all beneficial to accurate, high-quality channeling. The subject selection should reflect this need to maintain mental and emotional balance. Once you have learned the technique and can perform channeling accurately and smoothly, you can consider working with other contacts who may carry more emotional baggage. It is, however, important to learn the technique thoroughly before adding this extra burden.

For a beginner, the spirit contact should be a human or an animal with a well-documented life. This will provide a rich source of feedback information to check your channeling data against. This reality checking is vital to improve your channeling skill. The feedback session allows you to examine the accuracy of the information you perceived during channeling so that you can determine what is well grounded in reality and what is fantasy or error. Even for an advanced practitioner, channeling contacts whose lives are well known and well documented can, by means of the feedback session, help tune and strengthen the tenuous thread that connects conscious awareness to the deeper mind.

The third requirement in the selection of a good spirit contact is that the channeler needs to feel safe. If you feel like you need a barrier of protection from the entity, it is not a good entity to work with. In order to do effective and accurate channeling, you have to be in a fairly intimate, emotionally exposed situation with the entity. You have to be able to trust the spirit to handle that intimacy. Also, you will at times not know who you are channeling, as part of the process of learning about that entity and about channeling. There is no way around this.

It is something that you need to work through in order to achieve proficiency and accuracy. A basic trust between you and your spirit contacts is important.

For a beginner, down-to-earth, verifiable channeling sessions with spirits who have had well-documented lives should be standard fare. I would, for the beginner sessions, avoid cryptozoological entities such as Bigfoot and other creatures whose existence is not recognized universally. This also includes extraterrestrial intelligences, spiritual or religious figures who have a lot of mythology and belief baggage attached (unless there is substantial reliable historical documentation about their lives and actions), and mythological beings such as angels, demons, fairies, or djinn. You need to start channeling with human spirits of those who have died—individuals with whom you have no obsessive interest, fear, or attachment.

I realize that many beginners are motivated by the idea of contacting and communicating with extraterrestrial or mythologically based spirit contacts. I do not mean to suggest that a beginner must remain a beginner for years and years. However, you do need to have the channeling procedure memorized and to have gone through it at least a few times to be familiar with the communication tools to the point where you can use them effectively, and to feel comfortable with the idea that you may have incorrect perceptions in your sessions.

You need to be sufficiently detached from session results to be honest about feedback. This emotional detachment from both accuracies and inaccuracies should be attained before you attempt to channel a spirit about whom it is not easy to find real-time data for the feedback session, such as a figure from mythology. The detachment is learned when you realize that all sessions have both accurate and inaccurate information channeled. Once you understand this, and accept your sessions without being judgmental or egotistical about them, you will find greater spiritual growth and your channeling will improve in detail and quality.

Accurate results do not necessarily mean you are especially gifted at channeling. Neither do inaccurate results mean you cannot channel. The level of accuracy indicates only the presence or avoidance of belief and expectation biases. All human beings have biases, as it is a hardwired feature of how we process and interpret sensory information. It is important to accept this in order for you to progress in channeling skill and in spiritual growth in general.

If your emotions are out of control during the basic channeling session, you cannot work accurately when doing advanced practices, such as immersive settings, group work, front-loading, and trance channeling. The employment of settings in particular creates a very controlled emotional effect to encourage manifestations and add intensity to the experience. Practicing with pen and paper sessions while sitting at a table normalizes the channeling experience. Low-key sessions will help you gain confidence as well as settle any fears or excitement that may arise.

Begin by making a list of spirit contacts that include well-known historical figures, deceased relatives with whom you did not share a close emotional relationship, and animal species about which there is concrete information that can be researched. Avoid choosing close family members, since emotional attachment creates belief and expectation biases. As you advance in skill, you can add names of less well-known historical figures or relatively unknown nonhuman beings, such as angels, demons, extraterrestrial intelligences, and others that you are interested in, including closer family members. I encourage both the beginner and the advanced practitioner to work with a number of different types of spirit contacts rather than just staying with one contact. Different contacts will provide alternative perspectives on the information you are channeling.

The selection of a spirit contact can be related to topics that interest you. I believe most people have a number of questions they want to ask spirit contacts when they first get into channeling. The entities who demonstrate an expertise in those topics will be the first choice for channeling. Contacts may have special knowledge based on their life experiences that can provide interesting and helpful insights for the practitioner. Some of this special knowledge is documented in occult literature. For example, the airish spirits of *Steganographia* are said to be able to obtain information about the activities of humans at specific locations based on compass directions.

Let's use the angel Raphael in an example. Raphael is a mythologically based angel who is alleged to have very detailed knowledge of healing and medicine. If I wanted to channel a question about how to prevent cancer of the breast, I would not hesitate to choose Raphael. Consulting a spirit does not take the place of medical examinations or treatment, which should always come first.

But I believe that channeling can give hope in situations where hope has been lost and where human technology and medicine fail.

The selection of the spirit contact depends on your own interests. You can choose a contact by name, species, characteristics, appearance—whatever identifies that being in your mind. Contacts are chosen from history, your environment, dreams, literature, mythology, folklore, and other areas of interest. Some beings were part of historical events that you may be interested in, and if so, their lives can become the focus of topic-based inquiries. The grab bag questions will relate to the topic in which the spirit has expertise.

For example, if you are interested in the American Civil War, then a soldier or leader from that time may be a good source of information. Create a list of half a dozen questions to which you would like answers regarding the American Civil War. Word each question using the specific format presented in the next chapter. Put all the questions in the grab bag, then select one without knowing which question you have taken from the bag. Channel the insights the spirit may have concerning the Civil War. Perform a feedback session to verify or discredit the information you received.

I have a few suggestions as to what types of entities fit specific topics of interest. This is only a general guide. It is not exhaustive, nor is it set in stone. It is intended to get you started. Once you have gained a feel for the techniques, feel free to move beyond this limited list.

## Human Spirits and Ancestors

It is appropriate to ask these types of spirits about personal matters, money, family, relationships, living conditions, history, healing, biology of the earth, wisdom topics, concrete conceptual matters, and pre- and post-cognitions. (Precognition is predicting and describing future events, while post-cognition is describing past events.)

## ETIs (Extraterrestrial Intelligences)

Extraterrestrial intelligences can relate their planet's history and details of their lives, their biology, technology, wisdom, and methods of healing. Some have a talent for precognition and post-cognition. Since channeling can include planet-bound species, there is a huge potential for acquiring new knowledge regarding extraterrestrial technologies. In my work with these intelligences, I use the descriptions of the entities provided by witnesses when describing extraterrestrials who have made contact with human beings on Earth. I do not use the planetary names as given in some of the UFO literature (for example, Venusians, Pleiadians, or Lyrians), as there is a possibility of belief and expectation biases creating interference if you use the planetary or system names as species identifiers. This practice should continue until physical, astronomical verification of the inhabited, technologically advanced planet is made. Using the appearance and descriptions of the extraterrestrial inhabitants is a way to avoid most problems. This can also be done for other entities whose origins are uncertain, such as elves and fairies.

## Animal Spirits

Some of the areas of interest that can be channeled with this type of intelligence include Earth questions, questions about an animal's life, general healing questions, general wisdom, help in finding things, pet healing, and insight into an animal's behavior. Animal contacts can also give insight into sensory experiences that human beings cannot physically experience, such as an acute sense of smell. These heightened sense impressions include smell, taste, infrared vision, ultraviolet vision, sonar, and heat sensing. If the animal is extinct, there is also the possibility that it may have had a sense that we have not yet identified.

## Mythological and Religious Spirits

Mythological and religious spirit contacts can channel topics related to spiritual wisdom, healing, and history. Some can also manifest very powerfully and can help the channeler with difficult life situations. According to information I have received, a few of these intelligences are alleged to have somewhat limited knowledge about concrete places, events, and entities. This was noted in Dr. John Dee's diaries regarding the angel Nalvage. Dee asked Nalvage (pronounced "Nal-va-gee," with a hard *g* sound) about cartography, and the entity was either not able or not willing to answer his questions.[5]

---

5. Meric Casaubon, *A True & Faithful Relation* (London: printed by D. Maxwell for T. Garthwait, 1659), 153.

In my own dealings with these types of spirits, I have not personally found any deficit in their descriptions of physical locations and events. I have employed airish spirits, for assistance, in certain types of psychic work that relate to concrete physical scrying targets, and these entities seem to be able to channel that information accurately. Trithemius was also able to utilize these spirits for describing physical locations and events. These entities are strong in conceptual, precognition, and post-cognition abilities. As with extraterrestrials, if the entity has been known to have a physical appearance on Earth and its origins are not clear, a description of the species or individual can be used in place of a name.

## Your Spirit Contact List

If you are curious about a spirit contact, add the contact to your list. The contacts that work best for you will become apparent once you start channeling sessions. I have not had any issues at all with a spirit contact refusing to talk to me. If there is reluctance, then your focus will automatically go to an accurate secondary source in the Nexus. When I encounter this problem, the issue usually lies with my lack of focus, or the grab bag questions are not well worded. I think most spiritual beings who end up on your contact list will have in some way initiated contact with you. This is done at a subconscious level, so you may not be aware of it. Do not be afraid to do a bit of trial and error when working with these spirits.

Using the categories in this chapter, select a few spirits you have an interest in and would feel comfortable talking to. I suggest choosing four to six spirits to start with. Here is a sample list of spirit contacts:

1. Tyrannosaurus rex (dinosaur spirit)
2. Ulysses S. Grant (American Civil War general)
3. Great-great-grandfather (relative you have never met)
4. Johannes Trithemius (abbot and magician)
5. St. Joseph of Cupertino (saint and mystic)

The next step is to format questions for these spirits. The best way to do this will be explained in the chapter that follows.

# CHAPTER THREE
# FORMATTING QUESTIONS

The method of channeling in this book utilizes a practice called *hiding the target*. This is the term used in *The Art of Scrying and Dowsing*. However, the word *target* is not really an appropriate term for channeling. It is more accurate to say that you are hiding or occulting the *subject of inquiry*, which is the goal, question, or focus of the session. When a channeler practices hiding the inquiry, it is also called *exclusion*. This practice improves the accuracy of channeled information. Hiding the focus of the session from your conscious awareness during channeling eliminates some of the issues inherent in channeling that relate to belief and expectation biases, as was discussed in the first chapter. It is only after the session is completed that the goal of the session is revealed for the channeler to examine.

The grab bag is the tool you will use to randomize the questions you want to ask your spirit contacts. This small cloth bag will hold identical folded slips of paper, each with a different question written on it. You draw one of these folded slips of paper from the bag and set it aside in a safe place without looking at it. The channeling session is then completed using one or more of the techniques presented later in this book. Information is gathered from the spirit contact and written down or sketched to record it. Only after the channeling session has ended is the specific question you drew out of the grab bag revealed. A single question may be channeled over a number of days using multiple sessions if more information is desired. In this case, the question is revealed to the channeler only after all the sessions relating to it have been completed.

## Why Practice the Grab Bag Technique?

It is not a "normal" practice for channelers to try to hide the subject of inquiry from themselves. Why, then, do I tell you that you need to use exclusion?

One of the benefits of practicing with hidden inquiries is that it increases the credibility of the channeler. If the question is unknown to the channeler until after the session is over, there is less inclination to assume the channeler is slanting information to suit the question. The primary benefit of hiding the focus of the session, however, is to reduce the risk of belief bias and expectation bias.

These biases are a result of the normal mental process of analyzing, categorizing, and labeling input from both the physical environment and the deeper mind. From that categorization process we develop beliefs, which are organized to form rules. Beliefs and rules enable us to survive and to get along with other people. This is a natural and usually beneficial mental process that helps all animals, including humans, adapt to their environment. Expectations are developed in the same way. Expectations are anticipated events or anticipated responses and behaviors based on preexisting rules and beliefs.

This mental process is universal, from the most primitive creature to the most advanced. It is a hardwired survival mechanism. Even though this ability to analyze and adapt is important for physical survival, these natural mental processes lead to expectation and belief biases, which are the bane of scrying and channeling. These biases overwhelm the information being channeled through the deeper mind from the Nexus-based spirit contact. They occur when perceptions rise up into our awareness from the deeper mind without any external sensory stimuli to accompany them. This causes the information coming from the Nexus to be distorted by mental processing as it surfaces into conscious awareness.

When you hide conscious knowledge of the subject of inquiry and restrict your mind to perceive input coming only from the deeper mind, you derail the process that distorts perceptions coming from the Nexus. During channeling there is not much environmental input, so you work with only a fraction of the information you are accustomed to working with when you explore, understand, and adapt to the world around you. While interacting with a spirit contact, the natural mental processing always tries to fill in the holes created by the lack of external sensory input by adding to the deeper mind's information flow. To protect the mind, additions are automatically done so that the new information from the Nexus reinforces previously held beliefs and rules. The mind then uses these beliefs and rules to predict what the spirit communication should be. The result is a kind of feedback loop in which the channeler perceives their mind reiterating previously established beliefs and rules in place of any new information the spirit contact is communicating. New information does not make it to the conscious level when this happens. If any information from the spirit contact does surface into the channeler's awareness, it is distorted to comply with beliefs and expectations that have been previously established.

The information that is coming from the spirit contact is present, but it is overwhelmed by the data processed through the usual channels. This will be especially true if the spirit contact's communication contradicts the channeler's previously held knowledge and beliefs, or consists of information that the channeler is not able to understand. Mental processing puts what the channeler expects the spirit will say into a format that the channeler assumes is coming from the spirit. Sometimes false sensory experiences will accompany these distorted perceptions to create the impression on both a sensory and a mental level that the information is coming from the spirit contact. It makes the channeling experience seem very real, even if it is coming from the mind of the channeler.

The end result is a perception that is mostly inaccurate. This still happens when you hide the subject of inquiry, but to a much lesser extent. The information processing mechanism of the channeler's mind will still try to fill in the holes and force compliance with previously held beliefs, but if you hide information, the filler from the interpretive mental processing is much easier to pick out when you examine the channeling data against real-time information regarding the spirit contact and the topic. This is why I have beginners work with verifiable inquiries. You have to learn that this mental processing issue is real. You need to learn what your mind does before you can accurately channel what the spirit contact is communicating to you.

In order to reduce the severity of bias, your mind has to be forced to rely completely on the deeper perception information thread coming from the Nexus. That means you cannot allow yourself to anticipate what the perceptions should be or what beliefs the information should be compliant with. It is only when this blinder is in place on your normal mental processing that you have a fair chance of channeling accurate information. The usual result without the blinder of exclusion is a mulligan stew of fantasy, personal biases, and communication from the spirit contact that is now distorted significantly by the mental filler. I have found that this happens regardless of the channeling procedure. It happens with electronic channeling, scrying, mental channeling, deep-trance channeling techniques, and spontaneous events such as visions.

There is no way to stop this natural mental process. Tools such as meditation and trance may help you to become calmer and more receptive, but these exercises do not derail the information processing done by the mind. Exclusion bypasses some of the processing that causes issues with accuracy. When used in combination with careful question wording and a focus on sketching and descriptions, the result is a consistent improvement in channeling accuracy.

Meditation and focus exercises will not, in themselves, increase accuracy, but they are beneficial in other ways. Meditation is a healthy self-care practice that can be good for you mentally and physically. Trance channeling makes use of meditation and focus to deepen the channeling experience. Trance channeling will be covered in later chapters as an advanced technique. However, my trance method still utilizes the practice of exclusion. The reason I continue to practice exclusion when working with trance channeling is because trance does not eliminate the problem of belief and expectation bias. It enhances the vividness and emotional intensity of the channeling experience. The trance channeled perceptions are still distorted by the processing and interpreting of information. This is why front-loading (working with minimal or no exclusion) should never be done with trance work.

The only thing that seems to work consistently to short-circuit the analytical processing of information is to exclude knowledge that triggers this interpretive process. This is why I developed the grab bag technique for both scrying and channeling. It is a solution that is reliable and easy to use. I have structured my method in such a way that it automatically reduces belief and expectation biases, thereby allowing the opportunity for high-quality channeling to take place. Information is more accurate, and the channeler works at a higher level of proficiency. Channeling without knowledge of the goal of the session should be the rule of practice when seeking accurate information from spirit contacts.

## Formatting Channeling Questions

When you do channeling, you will be working with both concrete and conceptual questions. These are the two main categories of inquiry. A *concrete question* is a question that usually involves a location, an event, and entities. It is a question that can be answered easily with sensory-based information—something that can be seen, heard, felt, smelled, or tasted. A *conceptual question* is a question that involves meaning, thoughts, ideas, and emotions.

When you create your list of questions for a spirit contact, word the questions in a way that is specific, objective, clear, and open-ended. By open-ended, I mean that the question should not limit the amount of information the spirit wishes to communicate. A minimum of four properly written questions need to be placed in the grab bag. Including four unique questions creates a certain desirable level of doubt as to which question you have drawn from the bag. Having that doubt is what creates the exclusion effect. It enhances channeling accuracy. When working with broad, nonspecific topics, you can subdivide the topic into multiple specific questions, all of which go into the grab bag.

## Subdividing Topics

A general topic is divided to create questions that allow a thorough examination of all facets of that topic. For example, if you wanted to communicate with a spirit on the topic of world peace, you would divide the various aspects of that topic and make a series of questions about it. If you wanted to examine world peace in the future, you would divide it into questions pertaining to dates to be examined, the roles of various countries, the parts played by world leaders, quality of life, economic changes, and so on. The questions you create would each take one of these subtopics and be worded so that the subtopic, if drawn from the grab bag, becomes the session goal. Wording should be done in a way that keeps your session goal clear, concise, and precise.

Specific tasks for this example of future world peace might look something like this:

1. How much progress will be made toward world peace on December 12, 2050?
2. What are the roles of key world leaders in their efforts to secure world peace from 2040 to 2050?
3. What changes in the quality of life will affect world peace from 2040 to 2050?
4. What are the economic changes that will affect efforts toward world peace from 2040 to 2050?

Each of these questions looks at a very specific aspect of the overall topic of future world peace. The more precisely the question is worded, the better your channeling information will be. The subtopics in this example cover a wide range of desired information. This creates the necessary uncertainty as to which specific question has been drawn from the grab bag.

## Doubt Is Your Best Friend

When you compile questions for the grab bag, it is desirable to create a high level of uncertainty as to which question you have taken out of the bag. This can be done by having a variety of topics in the grab bag, with at least one topic that is completely verifiable, called a *calibration question*. The calibration question helps you ascertain any mental processing that is interfering with your channeling, and also helps you eliminate it. The presence of the calibration target in the grab bag creates a healthy and desirable level of uncertainty as to which question you have chosen for the channeling session. Doubt is the best friend of the channeler.

For example, you could add to the topic list above on future world peace "What did the winner of the 1980 US presidential election look like?" This was Ronald Reagan, for those who do not know. It is a very different topic from the future of world peace. If you have four questions related to future world peace, you add this calibration question on the 1980 US election to the grab bag. When you take a question out of the grab bag, you will not know if it concerns future events or this very concrete, specific, and verifiable inquiry.

You may be able to deceive yourself about the responses you channel for future peace, but you cannot deceive yourself about the appearance of Ronald Reagan. If you receive responses from your spirit contact about the future state of the world and then find you have drawn the calibration question about Reagan's appearance, it will bring you down to earth with a thump. When you know that this is a possible outcome going into the channeling session, it will create real uncertainty as to which topic you are channeling information on.

If you feel uncertain or blinded by this procedure, then the grab bag has successfully excluded the mental processing that can interfere with accurate channeling. When you first do this, it might feel very uncomfortable. The king of your mind, your usual sensory information processing pattern, has been shut out of the room and does not like it. The initial response to exclusion is protest from the king, so to speak. However, once you experience the magic of this system, you will not want any information to be given to you before a channeling session. Now we will move on to look at another issue that creates inaccuracy in channeling: the wording of the questions being asked of the spirit contact.

## Characteristics of Inquiry Questions

Let's take a look at the structure of inquiries. An inquiry is the written goal of the session. It is concealed from the channeler during the session, but even though it is hidden from the conscious mind, it will register at a deeper level and is not hidden from the spirit contact. It is very important that inquiries be written correctly, even though they remain concealed from you during channeling. Poorly worded inquiries can create significant problems in the session and can cause a session to go completely off track.

*1. The inquiry needs to ask for specific information that includes time and location, if they are relevant.*
If the spirit is asked to make a prediction, then the time and the place of the prediction need to be as specific as possible for that question. If time and place are relevant, they should be included in the tasking of the inquiry. Predictions are considered to be concrete and will include specific information such as time, place, and event. Some conceptual questions will not relate to specific times or locations. Conceptual inquiries that do not relate to time or location may involve ideas, opinions, function, or purpose.

## 2. Inquiries should be open-ended.

This means that the inquiry needs more than a yes or no answer. It also means that the question is eliciting a description rather than just a one-word or short sentence answer. Take another look at the calibration question mentioned earlier: "What did the winner of the 1980 US presidential election look like?" This is an example of an open-ended question. The phrasing of the following question is not open-ended: "Who was the winner of the 1980 US presidential election?" This question is forcing an answer instead of looking for a description. It is a closed question. The use of closed questions is a good way to crash and burn when channeling.

Using descriptions and emphasizing sketching will improve the perceptive accuracy of spirit communication and other divination techniques. When you have to write perceptions or describe sketches, you always need to elicit descriptions with the wording of your questions. A description contains shapes, adjectives, verbs, colors, and lines. Channeled descriptions are best documented by sketching. If you are asking for something that can be sketched or described, then your wording has probably been done properly.

The closed question elicits a label, and as you learn to channel, you will learn that labels (the name of a person, place, or thing) are very undesirable, as they result from the processing of information instead of originating in data coming through the deeper mind. Forcing the answer to be a label is trying to use categorization instead of channeling. Channeling, scrying, and other forms of divination do not work when you categorize, because that is the part of your mind that analyzes data and fills in the holes with belief and expectation biases. If you create a question that is asking for a label, you are trying to bypass the true channeled information coming through the deeper mind.

By writing open-ended questions, you automatically become open to perceptions from the deeper mind. This allows you to perceive information that contradicts what you believe or expect, and strengthens the communication between you and the spirit contact. Open-ended questions also allow for image-based transmission of information. The most accurate channeled data is almost always image-based. Natural primary telepaths convey communications in a series of images, with accompanying affective values, rather than using language and verbal descriptions.

Because of the way communication occurs between spirits and telepathic species, image transmission is always more important and more accurate in channeling than verbal descriptions are. It is the same with scrying. Normal mental processing translates this emotive imagery into language. By understanding that the descriptions you receive from spirits will likely be image-based, and by wording your inquiries accordingly, you will be able to comprehend the information from the deeper mind with greater accuracy.

### 3. Use direct, clear, and specific wording.

An effective inquiry will be written in language that is direct, specific, and clear. It will tell the spirit contact where they need to go and what they need to look at, and to communicate what they observe back to you. The directions for the contact have to be worded precisely and concretely—you cannot leave room for interpretation. Even higher spirits can interpret inquiries incorrectly. To prevent this from happening, always make the wording of the questions in the grab bag clear, short, and direct. You can do this even if you do not use specific times and dates.

Asking a spirit contact to examine an artifact is an example of using precise wording when you are not able to be specific about the date and time of the subject of inquiry. Let's say you want to examine a strange artifact that came from Iran. No specific date for the artifact has been determined, and you cannot tell by looking at it what its function was. You want to try channeling information from a spirit regarding this artifact. You can set your time by using such phrases as "when this artifact was best understood," "when this artifact was used by the ancient Persian civilization," or "when this artifact was made." You are able to make the location specific because you know where the artifact was found. The spirit who could answer all these questions would be any human or some of the religious spirits, such as angels. These would not be good questions for an animal spirit or an elemental, because insights regarding human history are more specific to a human being and, subsequently, a human spirit. The tasking questions could be:

1. What was the function of this object found in Iran at Zahedan?
2. Who made this object found in Iran at Zahedan?
3. Who used this object found in Iran at Zahedan?

4. What did the winner of the 1980 US presidential election look like? (calibration question)

Your spirit contacts have access to an unimaginably vast network of information. Remember, information access is not limited to the earth in the here and now, but includes all of this universe, all of the Nexus, all other universes, all times, all locations, all living creatures, and all events. If you give instructions that are too vague, it is like trying to find a needle in a haystack.

### 4. Wording of the tasking must be objective.

A *leading question* is a question worded in such a way that the respondent is forced to answer according to your beliefs and expectations. The opposite of a leading question is an *objective question*, which accepts possibilities outside of anticipated responses. Asking leading questions forces the spirit contact to comply with your belief and expectation biases in their channeled responses. You can actually insert your biases into your perceptions of the responses by the way you write your tasking inquiries. You then face a problem that is similar to the one you would have if you possessed prior knowledge of the session goal. You essentially defeat the advantage of hiding the inquiry by creating tasking statements that are leading. Objective wording is very important to the integrity and accuracy of the channeling session.

If you write leading questions that force the spirit and your own perception into false descriptions, it is likely that the contact will not tell you anything, and what you hear in the channeling session will be coming from your own mind. If that happens, the integrity of the session is lost. You will still perceive a response, but it will not be coming from the spirit you are communicating with or from the deeper universal mind. Let's take a look at a few examples of leading questions.

"When will the city of Tampa go under water due to climate change?" Why is this a leading question? We do not know that Tampa is going to go under water, that it will exist in the future, whether some other disaster will occur and destroy parts of the city, or if nothing at all will happen to it. To make this question objective you would write, "Where are the average seawater levels in and around Tampa, Florida, in relation to large structures present in the city on July 1, 2050, July 4, 2060, and July 6, 2070?"

"When will the Boston Red Sox win the World Series?" We do not know if the Boston Red Sox will ever again win the World Series, or even if they will exist in the future, or if the World Series will exist in the future. To change this question to objective wording, write, "What is the appearance of the uniform of the baseball team that wins the most important ball game of the year in 2023?" Be careful with annual events such as the World Series, as they may not exist in the future. For ball game predictions, I would not try to predict more than two years into the future for this reason.

"What kind of aliens built the Great Pyramid, and how did they do it?" We do not know if aliens physically contributed to building the Great Pyramid. To change this question to objective wording, write such questions as "How was the Great Pyramid built?" "What did the entities who built the Great Pyramid look like?" and "What was the construction process that went into building the Great Pyramid?" The best way to obtain new information about the building of the Great Pyramid is to ask the spirit contact to describe the designing of the Great Pyramid, the different roles played in its planning and construction, the obtaining of materials for building it, and how those building materials were put into place at the site.

"Who is the Beast of Revelation and when will he appear?" Revelation is a prophecy that was written in the first century CE. It has been the focus of endless speculation and interpretation in the Western world. We cannot be certain that the events in the biblical book of Revelation will ever occur or that they are future events. You are also combining two questions into one. This can be done effectively, but it is best to wait until you have some experience with channeling technique before you combine two tasks into one question. To change this question to objective wording, write, "What is the meaning of the Beast in the book of Revelation?" If the channeling session indicates that a future ruler was being symbolized as the Beast of Revelation, then further questions can be asked to clarify and describe that ruler. In this way, you are not forcing an answer that supports your interpretation. It allows for a more objective description by the spirit, who can access accurate information.

Wording questions in such a way that they make assumptions based on a preexisting idea or opinion needs to be avoided, so that the spirit contact you are channeling is not trapped into having to transmit information in line with your opinions. This will invariably lead to self-deception and fantasy. What's more, it will be destructive to your relationship with the entity. Writing leading tasking questions can have consequences beyond the individual session.

In summary, word your questions in clear, specific, and objective language. Even though these questions are hidden during the session, they will guide the spirit contact and your channeling to provide you with high-quality, accurate information. If you find during the feedback session that the information was inaccurate, you should suspect faulty wording of the question first, assuming you practiced exclusion and were not trying to guess what the session goal was. A badly worded question is like a crudely drawn, imprecise map. It is the most likely culprit if you find yourself led astray during channeling.

## Wording of Conceptual Questions

The examples so far in this chapter are concrete examples with very specific times, places, and objectives for the channeling session. Channeling is not always about a specific time, place, or person. You will, without a doubt, have conceptual questions as well. The wording of conceptual questions can be a bit tricky, so I want to go over this in some detail. Let's examine what a conceptual question is. A conceptual question is nontangible. It does not involve a specific time and place. It involves inner workings—thoughts, ideas, philosophies. Concepts are associated with physical things, but the concept itself is abstract and often symbolic. Here are some examples of conceptual inquiries.

### Engineering (How Is It Made?)

The spirit contact describes the construction and assembly of an object or design. The conceptual part is concerned with the engineering. This can be a physical object or an idea. It is the conception of a plan or an invention. Asking about how an object was made, or the ideas behind how something was designed, are conceptual inquiries regarding engineering.

### Mechanics (How Does It Work?)

The spirit describes the inner functioning of an object or idea, the steps that relate to a process, or the flow of energy through that process. "How does an electric car work?" is an example of a tasking question that involves mechanics.

There is a physical component to electric cars, but the concept or physics behind the flow of electricity is conceptual, and because electricity flow cannot be directly observed, it is also theoretical.

## Interpretation

Interpretation concerns the symbology, or meaning of the symbols, that are perceived and related by the spirit. These symbols can be alphanumeric, glyphic, or pictorial. That is to say, they can be numbers and letters, simple shapes, or images. This is a very good subject of inquiry for beginners because the information can be validated through research. The information can be completely verified, leaving no room for doubt as to whether or not you were able to perceive the spirit contact's message. This can also be useful for archaeology targets that contain information written in untranslated writing systems. "What is the meaning of the Hebrew letter *aleph* as it relates to the Tree of Life?" is an example of a tasking question involving symbology.

## Recipes

The term *recipe* is used here in its broadest sense and not just as it applies to cooking. When a spirit gives a channeler a recipe, they can describe healing formulas, techniques such as mantras or meditation, or trance induction. Spirits are also able to describe other recipes related to well-being, personal spiritual growth, and the use of magical formulas and techniques. These are examples of conceptual recipes that can be channeled from a spirit. An example of this might be "How can I make an effective talisman?"

## Inner Chemistry

Inner chemistry is a description of chemical processes, transformations, bonds, and formulas. It is a deeper, more esoteric type of chemistry than observable science. This is a new area and has not been explored much in channeling. Genetics and other organic chemistries have been the focus of the very few people who have attempted this challenging subject of inquiry. Description of the bonds between atoms is something that is not directly observable, but the information can be channeled. The spirit contact is not limited by the size of the object, so a description of chemical interaction can be obtained through channeling. A tasking question involving inner chemistry might be "What does the process of bonding between hydrogen and oxygen in a water molecule look like?" Note how the question elicits a response that is best represented by a sketch.

### Improvement of Channeling Skills

Using your channeling skills to allow the spirit to give recommendations for improvement of channeling accuracy and clarity should be standard practice for anyone working with channeling or scrying. No one can tell you how to improve your accuracy better than a spirit contact who is working with you. The inquiry "Describe how I can improve my communication with you (name of spirit contact)" should be written and placed in every grab bag that you create. It was through years of working with this inquiry that I developed my scrying and channeling systems.

### Causal Relationships

Spirit contacts can describe cause-and-effect relationships. This can relate to any process, including those in chemistry, geology, biology, medicine, and engineering. An example of this might be "What are the hidden geological, energetic, and Nexus-based factors that affect the frequency, severity, and timing of earthquakes?"

### "Why?" Questions

Spirit contacts can answer "why?" questions with regard to any topic. This is particularly true of cause-and-effect questions and human-human, human-nature, and human-spirit relationships. An example of this might be "Why do properly formatted predictions sometimes fail to be accurate?"

You now have an idea of what kind of conceptual inquiries we will be looking at when using channeling as a tool for uncovering the secrets of the universe. Channeling and telepathy are flexible skills, and this method is designed to be used for a wide variety of interests and needs.

## Sets of Inquiries for the Grab Bag

Here is an example of a good set of inquiries for a specific spirit contact, the Elizabethan alchemist and seer Edward Kelley:

1. How did you feel about the entities you channeled while you were working with Dr. John Dee?
2. What aspects of living with and serving Dr. Dee did you like best?
3. How can I improve my channeling skills?
4. What were the best aspects of sixteenth-century life in England?
5. What were your feelings about the rulers you were living under?
6. How did you develop your scrying work as a profession?

The questions work best when you use precise, clear wording. If your directives are vague, the responses will be vague. In terms of feedback, aspects of the last two questions are touched upon in Dee's diaries, but the information in the diaries is not as complete for those two questions as it is for the first two inquiries.

It is best if inquiries are custom-made for the spirit contact who will be responding to them. This next example is for an extraterrestrial I will describe as a member of a small gray-colored, bipedal species. This species is reported as being capable of interstellar travel and has had multiple encounters with human beings. I will make the list under these two assumptions. A list of inquiries for someone of this race of nonhuman intelligences might look like this:

1. What is your appearance like?
2. How do you perceive humans?
3. How can I improve my channeling with you?
4. What are the basic concepts of interstellar travel?
5. How is your craft, which has been seen flying in the atmosphere of the earth, constructed?
6. How does your culture compare to human culture?

This grab bag list is largely conceptual in nature, with very limited verifiable information available. This demonstrates one of the challenges of channeling conceptual questions: there is not always a great deal of verifiable data. In situations where you are asking questions like this, it is a good idea to run through a few concrete, verifiable subjects with this extraterrestrial intelligence first to make sure you are channeling accurately. The following short list of questions is good for doing reality-check sessions. You are having the contact describe things to you that you can use during the feedback session to determine your accuracy in channeling.

1. How does the Vatican in Rome appear on April 1, 1998?
2. How does Old Faithful Geyser in Yellowstone National Park appear on July 4, 2018?
3. How does the sun in our solar system appear and function?
4. What does the Apollo 11 landing site on the moon look like on July 20, 1969?
5. What does my house look like right now from the side facing the road (outside view)?

This grab bag contains all verifiable inquiries. These are all topics that the extraterrestrial entity described as a "small gray" is capable of describing and channeling to you.

I have never had any problem with an entity refusing to do a concrete channeling-calibration target with me. I get more complaints from spirit contacts I speak with that the information they channeled is not what the intended recipient perceived. Some contacts have disclosed to me that they find this frustrating. The idea of using calibration targets as a solution to this problem has met with a positive response from my own spirit contacts.

Finally, you should add a channeling improvement question to topic-related grab bags. This will allow the spirit contact to give you feedback on how you can improve the communication link. The question should be written in this form: "How can I improve my channeling?" This addition to the grab bag is an opportunity to allow the entity to help you. You should add this question to all topic-based grab bags.

You now have the essential information to write channeling questions. Good questions have to be planned out ahead of time. When you do your feedback session, it is important to see how the answers came across when compared to the questions. Doing this will help you channel more accurately. You need to make the questions appropriate for the spirit, and you need to have one calibration question for every four conceptual or esoteric questions. An esoteric question is a question that has two qualities. It is a question that relates to concepts such as spiritual matters or magick. It is also a question that cannot be physically validated through knowledge of history or through research.

For a beginner, it is best to do the first few sessions with calibration questions that can be verified easily. Doing this will help you learn how to channel and how it works for you. If you are an experienced medium, the principles underlying the practice of exclusion and question formatting still apply to you. The only difference is how you will perceive the information coming through your deeper mind. I would encourage you to try working with these techniques so you can see for yourself the difference they make.

# CHAPTER FOUR
# THE CONTACT RITUAL

Channeling is not just about obtaining information; it is also about making a personal connection. In order for a spirit you contact to communicate telepathically, or for an entity who is a natural telepath to establish a link with you, a connection has to be made on a personal level. How deep that personal connection becomes depends on the degree of trust that exists between you and the other. The purpose of the contact ritual is to help teach you how to make this connection. This ritual is done after you have decided on the spirit you will be channeling, made the formatted questions for the grab bag, and removed a slip of paper randomly from the bag and stowed it safely out of sight.

This contact ritual is also used to produce the altered state of consciousness needed for trance induction and trance channeling. I initially learned how to go into this state from the spirit of Edward Kelley, who gave me instructions via the radio—a scanning AM/FM radio. I was able to pick out his messages in the static and noise between the stations. He gave me directions and techniques that started me on this journey of becoming a channeler and scryer. This started in 2011. Since that time, I have developed that ritual further based on the Golden Dawn's Rising on the Planes ritual.[6] The visualization done during the working devised by the Golden Dawn was helpful in evolving an easy-to-learn contact ritual to use with channeling.

---

6. Israel Regardie, *The Golden Dawn* (St. Paul, MN: Llewellyn, 1989), 464.

The idea of rising through the planes is to meditate and allow your consciousness to rise until it reaches a refined state. Usually the seven chakras in the human body, or the ten emanations on the Tree of Life, are the symbols imagined in a progressive sequence for this. I first used this Rising on the Planes ritual for spiritual development many years ago, from 1999 to 2001. The feel of the contact ritual retains the same character as rising on the planes, but the visualization and purpose of the contact ritual changed over time until it evolved into the unique ritual I am presenting to you now.

The goal of the contact ritual is to help you develop an awareness of the spirit contact's presence and provide a sense of security while you are channeling. The sense of presence is a feeling you sometimes get when a spirit is present and connected to you. The experience is different from individual to individual and session to session. Sometimes it can be intense, and at other times you will not be able to pinpoint a feeling or sensation that indicates another presence is attentive to you.

## External Conditions for More Intense Contact

External conditions are the environmental factors that play a minor role in the intensity of the experience of the contact ritual and interaction with the spirit contact. The external conditions for more intense experiences vary, but generally the intensity increases in locations that appear to have features that connect the Nexus to the physical world. These geo-spiritual nodes are dowsable and believed to be along ley lines or at ley line intersections. Ley lines are alleged lines of esoteric earth energies that generally run in straight lines. They can be perceived consistently and appear to strengthen spirit apparitions and other paranormal manifestations. Religious structures and unusual land features are frequently near these geo-spiritual lines. Other than that, there is not much known about them.

If you want to have a more intense contact experience with a spirit or entity, you may want to experiment with such locations to see if they affect you. I cannot tell you for sure that you will have a more intense paranormal experience if you go to a ley line to do channeling or the contact ritual. I only say it is reported to be so by people I know who have interest in, and experience with, the paranormal. In the past, I have been asked to dowse ley lines because of this belief and interest by a local human-initiated extraterrestrial contact group.

External factors do not affect basic channeling sessions. The intensity of an experience is not related to the accuracy of channeling or the ability to channel.

Another factor is that generally you will have a more intense experience at dawn or at dusk. Traditionally, the *gloaming*, as the Scottish called twilight, when light and dark meet and merge into gray, is the time of day when spirits and fairies are most often seen walking the earth. It is a time of transition and also a time of balance. Direct light seems to be destructive to subtle energies in general. I usually work just before sunrise. Even though bright light is detrimental to certain types of paranormal manifestation, light level does not affect the ability to channel at all. The basic channeling session can be done at any time of day or night. It can also be done in less than ideal conditions, such as in a break room at work or in a restaurant.

The last factor I will mention is that electrical, cellular, and microwave impulses are destructive to the subtle energies involved in channeling. This is something that you can overcome with experience if the other environmental conditions are fairly good for the subtle energies involved. I personally find that cell phones are the worst culprit. I make it a regular practice to minimize my exposure to these adverse factors. These EMP (electromagnetic pulse) variations can cause minor issues with a basic channeling session. If you cannot avoid the presence of electrical fields, you can still channel, but it may take a bit more effort to get through the session. These are distractions that, if allowed to grab your attention, will create a problem with focus during the session.

Regardless of the intensity of the experience, if you do the contact procedure correctly, the spirit contact should be able to communicate with you. The intensity of the experience and paranormal manifestations are not indicators of the contact's ability to interact with you. Even if you do not perceive a strong sense of presence, you can still communicate and channel the spirit contact. You can do this regardless of the conditions. The factors I have mentioned here only enhance the sense of presence.

## Preparing a Safe Place

The first step in the contact ritual is to prepare a safe place where you can communicate with the entity. This safe place is in your imagination and emotionally merged with your physical location. Do not get tied up in the details of this safe place. I do not recommend that you try to hold an image of it in your head. The feeling of being safe is the goal. The idea is to reinforce whatever your idea of a safe place is by creating it in a consistent way, using the same mental pathway to generate a calm, positive affective atmosphere associated with your current working location.

To create the feeling, try to imagine an emotionally neutral and comfortable setting to which you will guide the entity. This setting could be a sitting room, a garden, or any quiet spot where you believe the spirit contact will feel welcome and comfortable. It should be something simple and easy to feel. The sense of safety and comfort is your primary goal. It does not matter so much what the visualization looks like, as the affective atmosphere is the first priority. You are guiding the contact to a safe haven where the focus can be on information channeling and interaction without having to worry about distractions or dangers. The appearance of the safe haven is not as important as the sense of security and focus found there.

Creation of the safe haven ideally should be done in a comfortable, private place free of distractions for the length of time it takes to do the channeling session. However, less than ideal locations can be used if you can learn to focus through the distractions. Your focus is what creates the right atmosphere. Learning to create a safe haven regardless of your physical location or circumstances is an excellent skill to attain. It takes practice and determination. Think about the advantages of being able to do unrestricted channeling. You can work anywhere in any circumstance, and do so with consistent accuracy and quality. It is a goal worth attaining.

You need to mentally superimpose the feeling of a safe haven over your physical location so that the physical location feels like the safe haven. Understand that the physical location will usually not resemble the safe place. Having a physically identical location and safe place will happen only if you have access to a physical place that meets all the requirements of a safe haven and is conducive to the presence of the spirit. The idea is to think of a familiar setting that you associate with learning new and interesting information. The association should be one of safe learning, a place of trust where you can relax and be yourself. It is a place conducive to contacting and forming a personal bond with a spirit contact. Then you superimpose that feeling onto your physical location. If your focus is powerful enough when you do this, others around you may sense it as well.

Creating a safe haven is the first step in building an *immersive setting*. This is the use of a setting to create a certain feel that deepens the experience with the spirit contact and increases the possibility of paranormal manifestations—apparitions, psychokinesis, atmospheric changes, healings, lights, UAP (unidentified aerial phenomena, formerly UFO), and so on. Many people who are interested in channeling are also interested in experiencing these kinds of phenomena. Learning to create an effective emotive atmosphere is the first step toward creating an environment conducive to that kind of experience. In the final chapter, I will go over this in greater detail in order to help you utilize immersive settings to your best advantage.

Because of the way the contact ritual works, especially at the advanced level, it is important to learn what your physical location looks like, from the vantage point of the air just above the physical location all the way to the view from the upper atmosphere of the earth. This means you should have physical images of your location from the air. If you cannot do this in your head or have trouble with focus, print a few images from different heights. Include images from altitudes of 100 feet, cloud level (about 15,000 feet), flight level (50,000 feet), and low Earth orbit (99 to 1,200 miles above the earth).

If you do not have access to these images, then do the best you can to visualize the images with the information you have. The imagery does not have to be perfect to work. As with the safe haven, the emotive atmosphere is much more important than the actual detail of the imagery. The advantage of learning to do this mentally is that it helps to intensify your focus and allows greater interaction of the spirit contact with the physical plane. The mental focus helps you associate the act of connecting to a spirit intelligence with the ritual you perform to make the connection.

There are two variations of the contact ritual in this chapter. I will go through the basic ritual first and then add the optional aspect of elemental imagery to it. If you feel uncomfortable visualizing the energies of the philosophical elements, the basic ritual is sufficient. To start with, if you find yourself having trouble visualizing something in your imagination, the best thing to do is to sketch each step on paper. The quality of your artwork makes no difference as long as the affective sense is maintained. Just do the best you can.

## Contact Ritual: Basic Version

This ritual helps you create an initial connection with a spirit by using a combination of physical actions coupled with mental visualization. It is done seated at a desk or table where you can do writing and sketching. I suggest you use a chair that has support so your back doesn't become tired. When you finish the contact ritual, you will move directly into channeling using automatic writing, as described in chapter 6. Once the contact ritual is completed, it is ideal if you stay settled in place and don't move around. The query you have drawn from the grab bag is put away in a safe place at this point. You have paper and pencil ready to go.

When you first learn this ritual, you should use a few material tools to help you get the feel of the procedure. Once you get a sense of how it works, you can discard the tools. While you are learning to make the connection with the spirit contact, it is important to use the same tools and the same procedure. Consistency will help you develop the mental pathways you need to utilize. This allows you to control the contact experience. It allows you to open and close the contact frequency at will. This is important to your development as a channeler. It is unhealthy to live with these contact windows constantly open or to have difficulty opening to the signal line to do a session. Learning control from the beginning will save a lot of misery if contact experiences become more emotionally intense.

You will need incense of any type you like and a candle—just a regular tealight will work. Light the candle and the incense. As the incense burns, you blow lightly on the rising smoke, using it to carry a message to the spirit. The content of the message is a gracious request to join you for a conversation. Imagine the smoke carrying the message to the spirit. Mentally reach out to connect to the spirit. Once you feel that subtle contact in your mind, use the light of the candle to guide the spirit to the safe place you have created in your imagination.

The sense of a spirit's presence is subtle. You are not looking for an apparition or other physical manifestation at this point. The sense of presence is a very delicate thing, and you will probably have to assume it is there a few times before you begin to understand what it feels like. If you work for about five minutes in the way I have described, you may make the assumption that the spirit contact has responded to you.

If, during the ritual, you feel something negative or a sense of being mentally pushed away, then stop the ritual. You can work with a different spirit or you can try again later. This is more than likely a result of anxiety on your part. Stopping the ritual will give you time to resolve what is troubling you.

The contact ritual will only take about five minutes. If you are in a situation where you cannot use real incense or light a candle, you can use a scent of some kind for the same purpose. The invitation will then be carried on the scent of the perfume, as it is on the smoke of the incense. I like using solid oil-based perfume. To make this, melt some soft wax (such as beeswax) or solid oil (such as coconut oil) and then add a few drops of essential oil. Do not put in too much oil or it will be overpowering. Add the oil to the wax once the wax is melted. Pour the wax into a small sealable container and use it only for this ritual by opening the container and allowing the scent to act on your mind in the same way as incense smoke. (The small glass containers that are sold with essential oils are an example of the type of jar I use for this.) It works best if you only use that scent or incense for the spirit invitation. Sound can be used in the same way as incense or perfume. I have a singing bowl that I find works very well. A chime can serve the same purpose.

If you are in a place where you cannot light a fire due to building regulations or other issues, you can use an electric tealight candle as a guide for the spirit, and it will work fine. I have worked with battery-powered tealight candles and there was no difference in my channeling session feedback results compared to the results obtained when using a flame candle. I find a live candle to be a distraction when I am channeling or scrying, so I started to experiment with the electric tealights and discovered that I was able to do the rituals using this device just as effectively.

The "reaching out" and "guiding back" mental focus should have a smooth and gentle feel. Forcefulness in focus and feel is undesirable. Being forceful may interfere with your channeling and communication abilities. Forceful action tends to be fueled by anger or fear. Both of these emotions will create a barrier that your spirit contact cannot penetrate. When this happens, you usually will end up channeling reflections of aspects of your own personality—your thoughts, beliefs, and ideas.

## Contact Ritual: Elemental Version

In this variation of the contact ritual, we will go a bit deeper into the Nexus. I will use symbols to help you memorize the procedure, which is also the procedure you use to work in trance channeling. Memorization of the ritual's essential components is necessary to be able to complete the procedures outlined in trance channeling. Literal belief in the existence of the philosophical elements of the ritual is not necessary in order to establish a line of communication with a spirit contact or to effectively use the ritual. The use of these philosophical elements is only a symbolic device to aid your memorization of the contact procedure.

The additional detail of this version of the contact ritual will help increase emotive intensity, and later it will help you with your trance work. The action involves rising through the astral planes mentally, going successively through each element: from earth to water, then to air, fire, and finally spirit. The elements are arranged in order of the heaviest (earth) to the lightest and most refined (spirit). The spirit contact's location is in the highest plane, that of the spirit element.

In this book I have used the five philosophical elements as a guide for this visualization since they are easy to understand and memorize. You do not need to enter trance for this. You will be sitting with your incense, perfume, or singing bowl in normal waking consciousness. You should be calm and focused on this process, without allowing your mind to wander to other things. If you have trouble with focus, it will help to physically remove any distractions.

To help you remember the contact ritual, I will relate the steps of the ritual in order as they are linked to the five elements. Using the elements as part of the contact ritual requires that you have a basic familiarity with their esoteric qualities, but it is more important to learn the feel of each element. Earth has to feel like physical earth for the ritual to have the greatest efficacy, air has to feel like physical air, and so on. Do not get too wrapped up in details. The ritual can be done without an extensive knowledge of what the elements are or where they originated. *Affect before intellect*—remember that and the ritual will be effective.

### Step 1: Earth Plane

Earth is the least active or energetic of the elements. Its nature is dry and hard, dark and dense, heavy and opaque. If released, it falls downward. It is the only element that possesses a fixed, enduring shape. A stone is a good physical representation of the earth element, but always remember that the elements are not physical substances but are the essential, fundamental forces and tendencies that underlie all material things.

Take a breath, then gently blow the message of invitation with the incense through the earth plane. Think of going through the roof of the building around you or rising toward the sky. You imagine in your mind that the smoke or scent is traveling to the sky. With your focus and imagination, follow the smoke out of the place in which you sit and upward as you detach yourself from the earth plane. Do not look for any particular sensations; just follow the smoke in your mind.

### Step 2: Water Plane

Water is heavy, cool, and wet. Like earth, water tends to move downward, but unlike earth, it does not retain its form but spreads itself, filling whatever channel or hollow can contain it. The shape of water is always changing unless it is confined by an earthly vessel. The natural tendency of this element is to flow and spread, and it is only at rest while contained. Uncontained, it will evaporate and rise, then fall again when it condenses. Material water expresses the key qualities of elemental water.

The water plane is related to water vapor and not a body of water. In your mind you are following the smoke of the incense through the clouds. Rise with the smoke, scent, or sound containing your invitation ever upward through the layers of clouds, rising steadily, with a gentle yet constant focus, calm emotions, and an openness to the spirit contact as you draw closer.

### Step 3: Air Plane

Air is light and active. It does not fall when released, but neither does it rise. It expands upward, downward, and to all sides to fill whatever space it occupies. Air not only is transparent, like water, but is also invisible, yet it can be felt in the form of wind when it is in motion. It is elemental air that gives the physical air we breathe its defining qualities.

The air plane is air with diminishing moisture moving toward fire. The physical location of the air plane is above the clouds or flight level for commercial jets and into the area of low Earth orbit in space, where the air is extremely thin. Elemental air is rarefied and pure, without water, and touched with the fire of the sun. You mentally rise and follow the smoke, focusing gently on the spirit contact with an open, calm heart. You mentally invite the spirit to join you. Your mind and the mind of the spirit are beginning to touch.

### Step 4: Fire Plane

Elemental fire is lighter than elemental air and strives to move strongly upward. Fire also expands more vigorously than air. It is dry and hot by nature, radiating heat. Physical fire embodies the essential nature of the fire element. If it has enough fuel, it will continue to grow vigorously until that fuel is exhausted. The most violent kind of fire is an explosion. All living things are vitalized by fire. The digestion of food is a slow burning and produces the warmth of life.

Fire is the last plane before spirit. It is a plane of radiant heat energy above the atmosphere and the source of all life in both the Nexus and the physical universe. The fire plane contains only a trace of physical matter. The sun burns with the lightest and rarest of elements, hydrogen. The fire plane is where contact with the spirit begins and the connection starts to solidify. An awareness of the presence of the spirit develops, and the contact in turn senses your request for interaction.

### Step 5: Spirit Plane

Spirit is the purest and most rarefied of the elements. It permeates the lower four elements and all material things, interpenetrating them. Spirit is often not included in the elements because its action is subtle and not readily apparent in the physical world. It underlies the structure of the universe. The nature of spirit is expressed in the material world by light, which shines out across space unrestricted by matter.

You are now in the Nexus. This is a place of transition where you can meet the spirit and the spirit can meet you. It is the access point to many dimensions, including the physical and spiritual planes. It functions as information storage and a transit point between the different planes and universes of the multiverse. The interaction is telepathic and the connection with the spirit is now forming solidly. You have joined with the spirit contact for the purpose of communication, and the contact is now ready to be guided to your location. As you enter the Nexus, you find yourself between worlds. The connection is maintained through mental focus, with calmness and openness. The right state of mind has to be maintained steadily during the return journey back down through the planes to your safe place.

### Step 6: Guiding the Spirit Contact to the Safe Place

Once you have made the connection with the spirit contact, carefully maintain your focus along with your emotional calmness and openness. The order of descent through the planes will be fire (space), air (upper atmosphere), water (through the clouds), and then earth (below the clouds to your location). The entity should be guided to the safe haven created in your mind, which is merged with your physical location. You have now successfully made an intersection between the physical world and the Nexus.

During your descent through the elemental planes, it is a good idea to continue to use the aerial view of your physical location as it appears in satellite images of the earth. This adds a visceral feel to the descent as you guide the spirit contact to your location. Do the descent fairly slowly to start with until you develop a good sense of connecting and guiding the contact back to your location. The contact and you both need to feel safe, accepting, and open for this to work. When you arrive, you should have an awareness of presence that you can associate with your contact.

This ritual does not have to be a long, drawn-out process. Five minutes should be sufficient to focus on the invitation in normal waking consciousness. The contact ritual should be done every time you are going to interact with an intelligence, regardless of the origin of that intelligence.

## Using the Contact Ritual

The more you do the contact ritual, the more effective it becomes. Both variations gain strength with use as long as they are practiced regularly on a weekly or biweekly basis. Neither variation works well as a one-time ritual. The cumulative effect is more important than the form of the ritual or the tools used.

You are not seeking a revelatory experience or manifestations with the contact ritual. Its effect is subtle, and the feel of it may seem rather mundane or even a bit boring after a few rounds with it. That is what needs to be accomplished. A sense of intellectual disengagement from the ritual is a good thing. Calm focus needs to be attained, so while the contact ritual is still a novel, exciting experience, you will not attain the level of focus you need to make the ritual fully effective. The full channeling potential is not realized until emotional neutrality is attained by the channeler. The only way to do this is through repetition. Eventually the conscious mind will lose interest and let go of its hold on your mental processes and emotions.

Once you have the variations of the contact ritual learned and can do them without referring to the text, you can discard the tools altogether. The tools are only there to help you memorize the procedure and enable you to viscerally generate the required affective atmosphere. You are always looking for a sense of presence and a sense of activity and energy as you move through either variation. Usually this sense is strong the first few times you do the ritual, and then it becomes more subtle. When it reaches the point where the sense of presence is subtle, the ritual has a greater effect. It does not matter which of the two ritual variations you use. Try both and use the one that works best for you.

I suggest working through each of these contact ritual variations a few times to get a feel for them before moving on. Work through them with different spirits. Become familiar with how the spirits feel when you contact them in the Nexus and when they are present in your physical location after the return journey. This is called a *sense of presence*. Each entity gives a different sense of presence.

In the Nexus, this sense of presence is the signature of the entity and is what spirits and telepathic entities use for identification instead of a verbal name. The sense of presence distinguishes one individual from another. You need to learn how to identify a spirit using this aspect of its personality rather than only its given earthly name.

I suggest that you work with a variety of spirits. Many channelers work with just one or two spirits over their entire lifetime. I think this practice is detrimental to spiritual development. The personality of the spirit can become enmeshed in the practitioner's own personality if a channeler focuses on that spirit too much. No one spirit can meet all of your emotional needs. It is important to maintain healthy boundaries both when working with the Nexus and in your physical life.

How much contact is too much is an individual determination. It is healthiest for the practitioner, and probably also for the entity, to keep a light hold on each other. Be friends and be loving, but do not cling or obsess. Rotating your channeling sessions with different spirits will prevent any issues with that. It will also provide you with a richer, more well-rounded experience. As you gain confidence and experience, you will be working with entities that are nonhuman in origin, as well as engaging in telepathy with physically living entities.

## Closing Ritual

After you have finished with your channeling session, focus on the spirit and express a feeling of gratitude and love. Then release the spirit by saying, "Thank you for your help. Depart in love, friendship, and with my blessing." Then you need to completely turn your mind to something other than the spirit and the session. A good way to do this is to get something to eat or drink and concentrate on what you are consuming. Exercise or other physical activity can also work if you focus completely on the activity. This helps to prevent residual contact with the spirit, which can be annoying both to you and to the spirit.

# CHAPTER FIVE

# CHANNELED PERCEPTIONS

In order to start to do automatic sketching and writing, it is important to understand what channeled perceptions look like. The perceptions I have already mentioned are best documented in sketches. In the first chapter I described how the mind analyzes information in such a way that it tends to drown out or overwhelm the more delicate communication that comes from the spirit through the Nexus. But I have not yet discussed what those perceptions are like. Let's look at the nature of channeled perceptions.

## Perceptions Are Subtle

Perceptions coming from the deeper mind are subtle. Channeling is subtle. In fact, I have found through my experiments that the subtler the transmission, the more accurate the information. This is true with both scrying and channeling.

The desire to experience spectacular supernatural appearances during channeling reflects a desire to be entertained. If you focus instead on accuracy, the information will be more specific and useful, and the risk of self-deception greatly reduced. The channel is like a fine gossamer thread extending through the raging river of your mind. Once you have a handle on what it feels like to connect with that thread, it becomes easier to find it in future sessions. It mostly takes some practice.

With practice you will also learn to quiet your thoughts. One of the benefits of meditation is that it calms that raging mental river and makes the fine thread of the signal coming from the spirit in the Nexus a bit easier to locate. Exclusion also plays a big role in quieting down the river of the mind. In fact, hiding the inquiry is probably the most important thing that can be done to help you catch hold of that subtle gossamer thread.

## Perceptions Are Descriptive

Channeled perceptions surface in terms of the physical senses, primarily as sights, sounds, odors, tactile sensations, and changes in affective atmosphere. This information comes forth as sensory descriptions, sometimes as symbolic images, abstract shapes, lines, movement, and occasionally lights. Verbal perceptions of the deeper mind will well up in descriptive terms, as opposed to labels or other interpretations.

Labeling is the mental operation of categorizing, naming, and processing sensory information. It is the result of interpretation, and only rarely will it relate directly to channeled information. Communication within the Nexus does not involve the use of language, which is a characteristic of physical beings. Even then, the majority of physical beings in the universe do not use it. On Earth, language is limited to a dozen or so animal species, including humans. Instead, the telepathic transmissions appear to the channeler in terms of sensory information, ideograms that are usually written in the form of pictorial symbols with self apparent meaning, and visual and emotionally based descriptions.

There is a tendency when channeling to interpret and label the information. It is during this process of interpretation that information is either lost or distorted. To help prevent this distortion, I encourage the use of descriptive language whenever you are either scrying or channeling. Writing down your perceptions in descriptive terms will yield more accurate information. Verbal descriptions and sketches are closer to the source of channeled information than are labels. Less interpretation is involved when working with descriptive language, and even less when sketching. The result is a truer accounting of the communication coming from the spirit contact in the Nexus.

An easy way to remember how best to employ descriptive language is to write using adjectives, verbs, and terms related to the senses, such as sight, smell, and touch. For example, you might use the terms "glowing, elongated, dancing, quick, bluish-gray" to describe the appearance and motions of a UFO, but you would avoid the terms "flying saucer, UFO, spaceship, aliens" because these are labels, the result of analytical mental processing.

## Labels Are Not Deeper-Mind Perceptions

A label is a name of a person, place, or thing. It identifies what that thing is, rather than describing it. Examples of labels are "house," "man," "woman," "cat," "bicycle," "tree," "alien," "Alpha Centauri," "ghost," "mother," "father," "angel," and "demon." As a rule, a label is not a direct perception but is the result of an interpretive mental process. This interpretation will overshadow the perceptive information coming from the spirit contact in the Nexus.

If a label appears during a channeling session in which exclusion is practiced, the source of the label is the channeled perceptions that have undergone mental processing by the channeler. For this reason, when exclusion is practiced in a session, there is a way to extract the channeled communication contained in the label. The label is like a fruit that contains a seed. The label is what you see in your mind when you are trying to channel, while the seed is the actual communication. That seed is a part of the package, but it is completely different in makeup from the fruit that surrounds it.

To help you get at that seed, whenever a label turns up within the session structure, it should be broken down into descriptive terms in order to uncover the actual perception that was transmitted through the channeling thread. Most psychics and mediums who develop a habit of using labels during their sessions will find that their perceptions deteriorate in quality and accuracy unless they also develop the habit of digging deeper past the label to reveal the original perception.

To break down a label in an attempt to discover where it comes from, describe the label in terms of the five senses, and also describe the emotive feel to it. For example, take the label "bicycle." I might describe it as "blue, with round shapes, triangular shapes, relates to movement with a whirring sound." The affective association would be freedom and enjoyment. When I do the feedback session, I usually find that at least part of the description of a label relates to the subject of inquiry in some way. It is not usually the label itself that is accurate, but rather aspects of the descriptions of the label that I came up with. The seed in that "bicycle" label might be the sense of freedom and enjoyment and the relationship with movement. The triangular shape and blue color might not be accurate in this case. The label symbolizes the true and deeper perception in some way.

## Channeled Perceptions Relate to the Physical Senses

Describe perceptions in terms of seeing, hearing, touch, smell, and taste. Some of the animal spirits will channel detailed information relating to smell and taste. Those perceptions may be so detailed and complex that you cannot make sense of them, even after you reveal to yourself the inquiry that you drew from the grab bag. You may also perceive information coming from nonhuman senses, such as heat sensing, sonar, and visual information that is outside the normal human range of vision (such as infrared or ultraviolet light). I recommend that you spend some time working with animal contacts and extraterrestrial intelligences who possess senses that you, as a human being, do not possess. It gives an interesting expanded perspective on the world.

## Channeled Perceptions Are Image-Based

Your perceptions should be sketched, even if you are not artistic and can only draw stick figures. Sketching is always more accurate than verbal communication, and is truer to the source. Entities from different dimensions or worlds understand each other on a level that is deeper than language communication.

The idea that channeled perceptions are image-based can be confusing at first. When I developed clairaudience, I did not realize that my own analytical processing of the communication was what I was hearing. It seemed very direct, real, and at times overwhelming. Over time I came to a better understanding of the ability that I had developed. I learned to trace the information to a deeper source. It was through doing this that I learned how channeling really works. It became obvious to me that the words were coming from the mental processing of the images forming in my mind during the channeling sessions.

I also observed in other channelers that the best information they received came in the form of sketches. The drawings usually contained accurate information, even if the post-session interpretation was inaccurate. Images with self-evident meaning are the universal Rosetta Stone. Visual mental imagery is the primary communication medium of the Nexus. Understanding how telepathy and spirit communication work, and how to use our native telepathic ability, is the only way we will be able to understand and interact with nonhuman species.

## Perceptions Relate to Emotions

Part of the challenge in communicating with nonhuman, post-human, or Nexus-based species is due to the emotional component in channeled communications being too sophisticated for language. Because of this, the emotional aspects of communication cannot be easily translated. We are trained from childhood to focus on language instead of the deeper-mind perceptions. This results in a focus on the interpretation of perceptions rather than on descriptions of sensory information. The consequence of relying on analytical interpretation of sensory information, instead of learning to perceive emotional and imagery-based nonphysical communication, is that we mistake the interpretation for the channeled message.

This issue may mislead investigators working with extraterrestrial contactees. Instead of looking at how a human being processes telepathic perception, these investigators almost always assume that the translation of an entity's communication into human language is accurate, when in fact the recipient's perceptions are mixed with and distorted by belief and expectation biases. The inevitable result is a misunderstanding of what the extraterrestrials are communicating to the contactee, or at best a partially accurate message. Even face-to-face contact with very powerful natural telepathic species needs to be validated in order to ensure the accuracy and integrity of the communication.

Examining telepathic communications reported by contactees needs to be changed in two ways. First, the focus needs to be on imagery and emotional content of the communication rather than verbal language. Second, a strict validation protocol needs to be practiced with all telepathic communications. However, I think we would benefit from moving even a few small steps in the direction of maintaining a stricter protocol for examining telepathic communications during a UFO contact event. My motive for suggesting this is only to improve the accuracy and integrity of communications with extraterrestrial species.

The emotional content of channeled communications is very sophisticated. It is an important component of telepathic communication. Emotions, imagery, and sensory experiences take the place of a physical language with primary-telepathic and spiritual entities. The sophistication of the emotional component of channeling can be very difficult to define in words. We do not have linguistic terms for many of the emotions related to us during channeling. One way to address this issue of describing something that is difficult to understand in verbal terms is to describe how we feel, and how we sense the other entity feels, about a particular idea being explored. Watch for affective changes in the spirit contact. The emotions that the spirit is emanating feel as if they are your own during telepathy. It feels like your emotions change and that they belong to you. You have to learn to focus on the spirit in such a way that you can determine the origin of the emotional perception. Some spirit contacts have a complex and unique way of communicating with emotions that can be hard for a human being to perceive and describe. With practice you learn to describe and separate your emotions from the spirit contact and to describe unique subtle emotional sequences.

Even when working properly with a focus on descriptive language, we may find that there are just no words, not even descriptions, for the communication that is being perceived. In this case, a symbol can be created to express what cannot be expressed in words.

This is called an *ideogram*. An ideogram is a quick sketch that is self-apparent in meaning. It is an idea-gram. Ideograms are a quick way of expressing nonverbal ideas. The primary definition of *ideogram* in the Merriam-Webster dictionary is "a picture or symbol used in a system of writing to represent an idea or thing but not a particular word or phrase for it." The system of writing is your intuition, and the sketch or symbol is mostly self-apparent. In the case of symbolizing a spirit, for example, it will be a symbol made while you are thinking about the spirit. Ideograms are good to use when recording intuitive perceptions, as they are basically symbolic sketches and are useful for describing conceptual ideas that come across as you are channeling. An ideogram is the written expression between you and the deeper mind. It is also the universal form of recording, just as telepathy is the universal form of communication.

## Perceptions and Ideograms

Spirits and telepaths often transmit images when they are communicating. When an image represents a concept, it is called an ideogram. Ideograms that come from a spirit contact are usually abstract and contain a great deal of information in a highly compressed form. They work in much the same way as a zip file on a computer. The meaning of an ideogram obtained in a channeling session is usually self-evident. It is often an identifiable object. If an image comes to mind, sketch it out regardless of whether or not it makes sense to you.

After the image is sketched, you make an emotional assessment of the drawing that is on the paper. You do this by asking two questions. The first question is "How does the idea represented by this sketch make me feel?" The second question is asked of the spirit contact you are communicating with: "How does the idea represented by this sketch make you feel?" Assessing the emotional atmosphere between you and the spirit requires that you examine both how the spirit makes you feel and how the spirit feels. It is how spirits "read" each other. In this case, it allows you to get a snapshot of the emotional atmosphere generated by the reactions and emotions of you and the spirit as you interact with each other and a target.

If the sketched image is a recognizable object, then it has been subject to some interpretive mental processing. Use the same procedure to interpret it as you would with any other label—that is, break the image down into basic descriptions of size, shape, color, animation, and so on.

Ideograms are useful tools, especially when dealing with emotions or sensory experiences that human beings do not have, such as a dog's acute sense of smell and the information that the dog is able to gain from it. An ideogram can also be used to represent a spirit contact who does not have a personal name.

## What Perceptions Do You Pay Attention To?

The way to overcome misinterpretations of communication with Nexus-based entities is to focus on describing the following perceptions, which are based on true deep mind communication. First, describe sensory input—sight, sound, touch, smell, taste, heat, and sonar. Second, describe emotions, especially those given in a subtle sequence. The third type of description is to sketch imagery that comes to mind during communication. If you focus on recording these kinds of perceptions, while excluding the goal of the session from your conscious awareness, you will have a far more accurate interpretation of the communication with a spirit contact through the Nexus.

## Replacing Topic Knowledge with Primary Perceptions

I hope that by now I have established my rationale for excluding conscious knowledge of the goal of a channeling session. In order to run a channeling session with adequate focus, a substitute has to be found to replace that knowledge. The idea behind using this substitute is that it allows you to maintain focus and gives you a secure feeling while excluding the knowledge that would cause problems with accuracy. The first way I do this is through the use of what I call *primary perceptions*, and the second way is through session structure. Next I will go over primary perceptions, and in subsequent chapters I will detail the session structures that I recommend.

Four basic primary perceptions are used to replace the content of the question that has been pulled out of the grab bag and hidden at the beginning of the session. The inquiry drawn from the bag remains hidden and is not revealed until the channeling session is finished. Since the question is veiled, something has to replace the focus. That replacement is called a primary perception. A primary perception is the first perception you receive, or the first communication that comes through the deeper mind. These perceptions can be divided into four types. The four primary perceptions will help you focus on the channeled perceptions and filter out any mental processing that inadvertently happens. If you have read *The Art of Scrying and Dowsing,* you will notice that *there are differences in the primary perception list for channeling.* This is due to the fact that channeling frequently deals with conceptual inquiries.

I have made a specific list of the primary perceptions that you will be working with when you channel. You need to memorize this list. The names of the four primary perceptions are *object, presence, activity/energy,* and *concept.* You can use the first letters of these terms as a memory aid: OPAC.

## 1. Object

An *object* can be any solid, liquid, or gaseous inanimate object, large or small. An object can be natural or it can be fabricated by an intelligence. Objects can also be liquids or bodies of water, such as lakes and rivers, or any geological or artificial feature. Objects can exhibit activity or stillness. They can have motion and flow. They can contain energy or discharge energy. Objects can be as large as the sun or as small as an atom.

The conceptual perception of *object* can also cover construction, which is the intentional conception and building of an object. It is a result of energy expenditure and intentional change by an intelligent force. *Object* as a concept is intentional, focused, usually planned, and often intelligent (although there are less intelligent entities that construct objects such as ants and termites).

Concrete descriptions for the primary perception of *object* are size, shape, purpose, texture, density, colors, smell, taste, sonar, heat, viscosity, and flow. Never try to name or label an object. Use descriptions at all times. If a name or label comes up for an object, then describe the named object.

Conceptual descriptions of *object* are purpose, replication, construction, meaning, activity, and emotional response.

## 2. Presence

The primary perception of *presence* indicates that the designated location has intelligent, self-aware beings present. Further description of these beings can yield information as to who and what they are. When you are channeling, you will usually have *presence* as a primary perception since you are focused on communication through channeling. Usually there will be *activity/energy* that accompanies a primary perception of *presence*. There is a certain flexibility in this primary perception, depending on the belief and culture of the practitioner. In certain cases it may indicate other life that is not intelligent or self-aware.

Concrete descriptions of *presence* are size, shape, sounds, colors, smell, heat, sonar, and taste.

Conceptual descriptions of *presence* are emotional effect, relationship, purpose, activity, energy, meaning, and position in terms of authority or relationships to others.

### 3. Activity/Energy

*Activity* and *energy* describe movement, activity, ambience, and purpose. The *activity/energy* primary perception is often perceived because of the activity and purpose of an intelligent entity at the location. *Presence* and *activity* are often closely associated. The perception of *presence* is rarely read without *activity*. *Activity* can also describe physical force used to create change or can be a characteristic of the Nexus to create change and transition. It can be a specific physical energy, esoteric action, movement, or intention, or a characteristic of the Nexus that results in movement or transition. *Activity* can also indicate energy flow, aura, dispersion, concentration, and other descriptions associated with energetic flow.

Concrete descriptions of *activity* are direction, purpose, number, speed, colors, ambience, composition, smell, heat, and taste.

Conceptual descriptions of *activity* are purpose, emotional response, ambience, cause, result, initiation, and goal.

### 4. Concept

The formation of ideas, sequences, thoughts, and plans is a specific branch of the *presence* perception. *Concept* will not occur without the primary perception of *presence*. The *concept* perception involves subtle changes in mentation related to environment and interaction. *Concept* is also a part of the emotional perception usually of a location or other presence. *Presence* must be there for *concept* to be a primary perception. It is possible that the concept involved may be something that you have no personal experience with. If the channeler feels this is the case, then an explanation of the meaning of the emotion needs to be requested of the entity.

*Concept* description cues are type, change, frequency, prevalence, relationships, ambience, cause, outcome, purpose, emotional, and activity.

*Alphanumeric* is a specific type of *concept* that bears mentioning. The primary perception is *concept*, but the visual appearance when examined by the spirit will be alphanumerical. The appearance of alphanumerics that turn up in a session relate to *object* because it is a visual appearance, and they also may relate to *concept*, as the alphanumeric contains meaning and purpose, especially in cases of non-phonetic writing.

*Alphanumeric* description cues are appearance, shape, size, meaning, purpose, and emotional emanation.

When you start a channeling session, you may want to take these concrete and conceptual descriptions of the four primary perceptions and keep them next to you to help you know what questions need to be asked. I find this helpful to do. It prevents the feeling of not knowing what to ask next or getting stuck.

## Primary Perceptions and Feedback

The feedback session is one of the main tools I use to improve my scrying and channeling ability and assess how well I am doing. The general idea of a feedback session is to take the perceptions you came up with during the channeling session and study them against known reality. If you are working with an inquiry where the spirit can describe physical features such as activity and objects, then go through the spirit contact's descriptions one at a time to determine if the information channeled is accurate. Note the ones that you channeled correctly.

Perceptions that you cannot verify are ignored. It is important to celebrate successful perceptions and ignore the ones that are not verifiable. You need to allow your mental energy to be attracted to the accurate perceptions without punishing yourself for the inaccurate ones.

Judgmental and critical energies are detrimental to free, unbiased communication with spirit contacts. It is important to avoid exposing yourself unnecessarily to the opinions and judgments of other people. I suggest strictly limiting commentary or discussion on your perceptions, especially as you are establishing confidence.

Feedback sessions need to be done as soon after channeling as is feasible. Any time a future prediction is made, you must mark the date and time of the prediction and then do a feedback session after that time has passed. If the prediction is generic, it should be ignored as the result of belief or expectation bias. An example of a generic prediction would be "A big disaster is going to occur soon." Only predictions with dates and times should be recorded for eventual feedback.

Because you need to maintain an accurate record of feedback, you should keep a notebook with all the session and feedback information. Documentation is important when you are learning how to do channeling. It helps you to track your progress and identify belief and expectation biases when they turn up in a session.

# CHAPTER SIX

# TECHNIQUES FOR SPIRIT COMMUNICATION

In this chapter I will teach you specifically how to channel a spirit or a telepath. The basic technique used is automatic writing and sketching, which is the backbone of my channeling system. The alternative techniques of dowsing and the spirit communication board will be covered in the next chapter. I encourage you to practice channeling regularly. The more often you practice channeling, the better you get at it.

## Expectations

Channeling using the techniques described in this book will provide you with accurate information from spirit contacts. It does not require any special talent to do this. I am a firm believer in universal talent. All human beings are spiritual beings and therefore have the inherent capability to interact with spirit contacts by using telepathy and to perceive with nonphysical senses. These are not characteristics of just human beings. Many higher animals exhibit these abilities as well.

I want to draw a distinction between the subjective experience of channeling and the objective quality of communication achieved with a spirit contact. Over the decades, the experience of channeling itself has become the measure of both the channeler and the channeling session. However, the richness of the experience when interacting with a spirit has no direct bearing on the accuracy and value of the information received. Like most people, when I began to channel, I focused on the experience itself, believing that the more complex and immersive the experience, the better the quality of the channeling session. This error of expectation led to frustration. Even though I was getting rich emotional and sensory experiences, the accuracy of the actual information communicated was unreliable.

The breakthrough finally occurred several years ago when I realized that I was focusing my attention on the process rather than on the result of the process. Since that time, I have developed intuitive techniques that utilize improved traditional channeling methods without taking away from the experience that tradition offers. What do I mean by improved traditional techniques? I mean that the traditional skills of scrying, channeling, dowsing, and other forms of divination, along with magical techniques, have been improved through study and experimentation. I worked to optimize the accuracy of the information perceived using magical techniques to improve the reliability and quality of the desired outcome. I then broke down these improved techniques into a simple session structure that is easy to teach and learn, and tested it for consistency of flow, effectiveness, and accuracy.

Basic channeling for the purpose of communication with a spirit contact is a fairly mundane sort of experience. You are going to sit with a pencil and paper and write down or sketch the spirit's responses that are being transmitted through the Nexus. Without the incorporation of elements of setting—that is, creating a special environment in line with the type of channeling you are doing—channeling by itself is quiet, peaceful, and almost boring. It is the same sort of quiet focus that you use when doing math problems (but hopefully minus any tears of frustration).

The experience of channeling becomes more interesting when you start working with immersion in a setting designed to create an emotional effect. Heightened interest can help to sustain your focus and purpose, as well as being more fun. This is why I incorporate setting elements into channeling as a more advanced skill. However, you need to learn how to do basic channeling first before you can work with immersive settings. In the remainder of this chapter, I will describe the various techniques you can use for basic channeling.

The automatic writing session will consist mostly of a series of sketches. I cannot emphasize enough that the highest priority should be given to sketches when you are channeling a spirit contact. The product of an automatic writing session looks almost like drawings done by preliterate children of about four or five years of age. Preliterate children will draw things they see, hear, taste, smell, feel, and experience to express themselves. Their drawings are primitive and naturally symbolic, using ideograms that have self-apparent meanings. As they develop manual dexterity skills, children will also use three-dimensional modeling with Play-Doh or modeling clay. Using a physical medium such as modeling clay when channeling is very acceptable and helps you gain detail.

The art medium you use for your automatic writing and sketching sessions is up to you. If you are out in the woods, consider doing sessions with only natural materials. Examples of this would be making lines in the sand on a beach or sketching on rocks with burnt sticks (something that will wash off easily in the rain). This activity is an enjoyable, viscerally satisfying variation of the automatic sketching technique. There are many creative ways to use this skill.

During a channeling session, I have you sitting at a desk with a pencil and paper because it can be done this way almost anywhere. It is not dependent on location or weather. It is also easiest to work with tabletop sessions in a group setting. Channeling becomes focused on accuracy instead of dramatics, paranormal phenomena, and expensive tools.

Sitting at a desk with pen and paper helps to normalize the channeling experience. By *normalize* I mean that the experience of channeling becomes an everyday activity rather than something that requires a special setting and highly talented individuals. Every person on the earth can do this form of channeling if they want to. It is just a matter of understanding how the process works and doing a bit of practice with techniques that are designed around how the human mind processes and analyzes information.

The way I work with channeling today is a bit different from what has been commonly taught in the past, and is also different from what I described in my first book, *Spiritual Alchemy* (Llewellyn, 2016). Since then, I have continued to develop my skills in spirit communication. Both my scrying and my channeling have a higher degree of accuracy and efficiency than when *Spiritual*

*Alchemy* was written. However, the principles that you learn for channeling in this book can also be applied to the electronic spirit communication techniques written about in *Spiritual Alchemy*.

## Automatic Writing and Drawing

This is a traditional technique of spirit communication that was developed during the nineteenth century within the Spiritualism movement. You allow the spirit to channel information through you as you write and sketch your perceptions on paper or other media. It can be done freehand or through a spirit communication board. Because I emphasize sketching over writing, I generally only use the spirit board for one-word clarifications. The board is slow and not as accurate in practice as working freehand, with the channeler focused on sketching. Speed is important when you are doing automatic writing and drawing, and with channeling in general. The more quickly you respond to intuited perceptions, the less time there is for your analytical mind to step in and take control by imposing its belief and expectation biases.

Because automatic writing is quick and easy to learn and use, and has flexibility in terms of how it may be used, I have chosen it as the primary technique to work with in this book. It is done in normal waking consciousness. You do not have to be in a trance. It can be done anywhere as long as you have paper or something else to record the information on. It is also a good stealth method for those who wish to practice in less than ideal places, such as a break room at work.

I will be teaching you the most basic form of automatic writing, an intuitive method where you use paper and pencil, working freehand. The technique is called *trigger and response*. It is a simple, consistent way to practice automatic writing.

### Step One: The Trigger Statement

The first step with automatic writing is to use a trigger. A trigger is a command, or imperative statement, where you ask for a description during the channeling session. The trigger works better if you use the imperative form (a command) rather than the interrogative form (a question). The imperative form is precise and will state exactly what you want it to say. It helps draw the focus of the communication away from labels and biases.

The basic trigger statement starts with the word *describe*. You are using the imperative form of speech to open your side of the channeling thread between you and the spirit contact or telepathic entity. The use of an imperative statement affects your mind and imagination in ways that resonate in the Nexus. The spirit contact sends the information in a form that is much like a zip computer file. Some people call this a download. Your perceptions are a result of an information package sent by your spirit contact in response to your request. In my experience, sending this download is the technique that most contacts use to convey information about a topic. As the receiver of this data file, you have to unpack the information in an organized fashion.

Using the word *describe* as the primary trigger word for automatic writing opens that part of the interactive information package specifically related to the wording of the trigger statement so that you can get at the data inside it. Using the imperative *describe* helps to prevent trouble with labels and other bias issues. This is why *describe* is the first word of your trigger statement. You finish the trigger sentence by saying what you want to have described.

The first trigger in a session will always be "Describe the primary perceptions relevant to this inquiry." This is an example of how a trigger is worded, as well as how you open the channeling session. *Describe* is the first word of the statement, followed by the information you want to perceive, which is the *primary perceptions relevant to the inquiry*. This will be the most basic trigger in your automatic writing session.

The *response* is the second half of the trigger-and-response method of automatic writing. The response to this first trigger will be one or more of the four primary perceptions: *object*, *presence*, *activity/energy*, and *concept*. After you state the trigger, you then immediately write down the first thing that comes to mind. If it is just one of the primary perceptions, you write down the one that comes to you. If all of them come to mind, you write down all four. Also, you can have more than one of each of the primary perceptions. So if you begin the session with the trigger statement "Describe the primary perceptions relevant to this inquiry" and the first thing that comes to you is an activity and three objects, that is what you write down on your paper.

In addition to using this trigger statement at the beginning of the session, you can always go back to this trigger and uncover more primary perceptions.

This procedure can be done at any time throughout the session. So if you start out with "Describe the primary perceptions" and the response is two objects and a presence, you should then move on to describe in detail these three primary perceptions, working with them one at a time, still using the trigger-and-response technique. After you finish the first three primary perceptions, if you still want more detail about the inquiry, you can go back to the trigger you used to open the session: "Describe the primary perceptions relevant to this inquiry." Repeating this initial trigger may yield additional primary perceptions. You then work through that set of primary perceptions one by one until you finish obtaining descriptions of them. You can continue this process indefinitely.

The trigger statement that opens the session regarding the primary perceptions will be the *only* trigger in the session that requires a written response instead of a sketch. When you move on to each of the primary perceptions that were given to you during that initial response, you will then try to sketch, with as much detail as possible, the description you perceive of that primary perception. It is only with the first basic trigger, where you are looking to identify primary perceptions, that you write instead of sketch. It is very important that you understand this distinction. Any time you use the trigger "Describe the primary perceptions relevant to this inquiry," you will write down the relevant words from the list of the four primary perceptions: *object*, *presence*, *activity/energy*, and *concept*. Some may occur two or more times. When you go into detail about each individual perception that is written down, you will then need to sketch the details of that primary perception.

Once you have the basic primary perceptions from the first trigger statement, you need to unpack more detail about each individual perception. Triggers that are used after the basic session-opening trigger will always relate to the primary perceptions. I have a few guidelines to help you understand how to write the triggers. It is best if you write everything down, rather than merely speaking or thinking the triggers. It makes it easier to do feedback, and it also gives you information that can be compared to other sessions.

*1. Triggers start with the word "describe" and are specific, direct, and focused.*
Sticking with this formal structure will help you avoid confusion and lack of clarity in the responses you receive by making crystal clear to yourself exactly what information you are seeking. Remember, triggers are designed to open a package sent by the spirit contact. It is up to you to ensure that the package is opened and perceived correctly.

*2. Triggers should be objective.*
You are looking for objective information from the spirit, and the wording of your triggers must reflect this purpose. Subjective information is open to interpretation; it is vague enough to be essentially useless and should be eliminated by wording your triggers in concrete terms. There may be exceptions when dealing with conceptual primary perceptions. Even with a conceptual perception, trigger wording should be as concrete as possible. Reduce or eliminate the use of such equivocal words as "maybe," "should," "believe," "wish," "hope," "like," "prefer," and so on.

*3. Leading statements should be avoided.*
Recall the instructions on formatting grab bag questions in chapter 3. Trigger statements should never force the response to be in line with your previously held beliefs and expectations.

*4. All triggers relate to the primary perceptions.*
These basic perceptions take the place of the subject of inquiry for the entire session. For example, suppose a contact indicates that it travels in the physical universe, and you word the inquiry to ask how it travels. The inquiry is hidden from you—you do not know that you have drawn it from the grab bag. In session, you trigger the first statement to yield the list of primary perceptions. The response is *activity* and *object*, which are related to each other. You create a new trigger statement to perceive the description of the object and activity. The wording would be "Describe the object that is associated with this activity." The trigger should be completely focused on the primary perceptions. If you do that, you will avoid most of the problems with bias, and the session will be well focused.

*5. Triggers should always elicit a description and not a label.*

This rule includes the practice of asking the spirit for labels, such as its name, the names of objects, and other presences. Asking for a spirit's name is done frequently in ghost-hunting reality television shows. It is a common mistake in channeling that inevitably leads to belief and expectation biases. Asking a spirit for its name is based on the belief in magic that if you know the name of a spirit, you have control over it. However, many spirits do not use personal names. Verbal language is not characteristic of telepathic communication. Because of this, I suggest setting the belief bias aside that names can be used to control spirits. Avoiding labels will give you a more accurate picture of the spirit's identity and other important perceptions.

If a spirit's name is already known to you, I do not think it will be too problematic to use it. However, you need to be aware that the name you use may not have any relationship to how the spirit identifies itself, even if it is a deceased relative. In a channeling session, you do not want to be in the habit of trying to obtain labels, as this creates a problem with accuracy. This is why I suggest using a sense of presence to identify a spirit rather than a name, if the name is not already known. It is more in line with how spirits identify each other, and it stays away from the kind of mental processing that is detrimental to channeling accuracy. An example of this would be an animal spirit. Animals, with the exception of cetaceans and some bird species, do not use verbal names. Channeling to find a name for such a spirit would not yield an accurate identification.

*6. Triggers should not attempt to elicit a "yes" or "no" response.*

The only exception to this rule is if you are dowsing for a clarification on a previously given description. The problem with yes-no triggers is that they may force you to falsely perceive an inaccurate response, or force you into expectation bias even when the primary inquiry is hidden from your conscious knowledge. There is a strong instinctive pull to interpret and process the channeled information. Hiding the inquiry prevents the worst of it, but it can still sneak its way into session data. Wording your triggers properly will help guard against these unwanted mental intrusions.

*Step Two: The Response*

The response is the second part of the automatic writing technique of trigger and response. The response is what you write down after you write the trigger statement. With the exception of the first trigger in a session, which is limited to a response containing the four primary perceptions, the responses are sketched as much as possible.

The response is the first thing that comes to your mind and imagination after you write down the trigger. This response comes through within five seconds after you finish formulating the trigger imperative. It may take longer than that to sketch the response, but the images will be in your head within that time frame. If it takes longer than five seconds to receive the response, you have missed it. This happens occasionally, and the best thing to do is stop, take a break, move around to clear your head, and try again. When you do this, you do not need to repeat the contact ritual. Just refocus for a few seconds and contact will be reestablished. As you gain experience, you will be able to extend the time you use to respond to the trigger questions a little bit. However, regardless of experience level, the response to the trigger question should be less than thirty seconds.

The reason why the best response is always so fast is that spirit contacts can respond instantly and completely to a request. They can work faster than you can process information. Time is completely irrelevant in the Nexus. It does not exist. You need to grab that first impulse coming in because if you do not, your mental processing and interpretation mechanism will start to interpret the data flow, and you do not want that to happen. You want to hang on to the first thing that comes up that line, even if you take a minute to get it down on paper.

If you have a complex response or are a slow writer, it is okay to take longer to write it down. The five-second time limit is for perceiving the response and starting to write it. The idea here is to perceive the response and write or sketch it as quickly as you can. If you are inexperienced with this technique, a quick response speed (keeping it within the five-second limit) is more critical in preventing mental distortion and interpretation of the spirit contact's response. Once you learn what the response feels like, you can slow down a bit.

I have been somewhat of a nag about the importance of sketching. It is ideal if you can draw a series of sketches instead of writing verbal responses. If you put into practice only one thing from this book, it is to do channeling, scrying,

Tarot reading, rune reading, and all other types of divination with sketching rather than writing. The sketches do not look pretty when you are responding quickly to a trigger. Do not worry about their artistic value. Mark them down, then clean things up later.

Automatic sketching and writing are very similar to internal scrying, which is covered in *The Art of Scrying and Dowsing*. There are a couple of differences. First, the primary perceptions for channeling are focused more on conceptual ideas than concrete targets. Second, automatic writing is focused on interaction with a specific spirit contact or telepathic entity. When you do trigger-and-response automatic writing, you are perceiving information from a being and not connecting directly to the site of interest. Channeling gives you a different perspective of a location or event. There is a difference in the character of information, especially with the depth and conceptual or abstract components of an inquiry.

In both automatic writing and internal scrying, your attention is turned inward, and the information you perceive comes through your mind and imagination. When channeling, there is a spirit contact involved in the process of perception. When using internal scrying, you use your deeper mind to look directly at a target. The scrying session objective has a basis in time and space. Conceptual Nexus-based scrying is done in occult circles, but it is a small part of the art of scrying. Ideas, beliefs, and personality attributes are nontangible perceptions that are frequently seen in channeling sessions.

You do not need to have any particular beliefs as to who or what the spirit contact is. Automatic sketching and writing work without regard to philosophy or faith. To be honest, we really do not know who or what we are channeling. I think the best way to look at the mystery of the Nexus, spirits, and telepathy is to practice and observe. The rules fall outside known science and physics, so that knowledge is not going to help us understand channeling at this point. We have to learn a new set of physical laws when dealing with the Nexus. We are still in the Stone Age when it comes to understanding the basic principles that govern that universe.

## Automatic Writing

To have a successful automatic writing session, you need to make yourself very quiet and attentive, in both body and mind. The experience of a spirit contact channeling through your deep mind is subtle. It feels as though you are making it up. It does not feel distinct from other forms of thought and imagination that you experience every day. At first, it is a little hard to believe you are channeling. In spite of the rather mundane nature of the experience, the information you perceive is real, and if you follow the directions, it will be fairly accurate.

We have all seen movies and other dramatic productions where the medium says her hand is possessed by a spirit. Often she will begin to move it around violently and start to scribble across sheets of paper. I do not discount the possibility, but this has not been my own experience with automatic writing. My sessions of automatic writing are loving, peaceful, and calm. There is nothing violent, disruptive, or dramatic about them—that is, not until I look at the results. On good days, the accuracy is startling, even after doing this for a number of years.

The trick to doing automatic writing is to not think about what is going down on the paper. You need to work quickly, almost reflexively. Your inquiries, framed in the form of imperative directives or commands, will trigger an instant response, which you must write down immediately without considering it. When I channel, the process is write the trigger and then sketch the response as quickly as possible. The two most important things to remember when doing automatic writing are to work quickly and to understand which triggers to put to the spirit contact that will yield the best information. Following the directions in this chapter will put you on the right path to perceiving good information in detail.

When you start to work with automatic writing, you may notice some initial resistance, a feeling as though you are being blocked. This is due to effective exclusion (the hiding of the inquiry), which creates that "talking to the wall" sort of feeling when you first experience it. The unpleasantness goes away with practice. You are likely to see accurate data, even with your very first session. The detail of the channeled information will improve as you become more comfortable working with exclusion.

Some of this unpleasant "talking to the wall" feeling is due to a fear of making mistakes. It is important to accept that you will have inaccuracies in the channeled information and be okay with that. Once you get over that fear, it becomes much easier to channel. What do you have to lose? If you have inaccuracies, it means that you have beliefs and expectations. It also can mean that you are being honest with yourself. It does not mean that you cannot channel.

When you do receive your responses, sketch and write down everything that comes to you. The main focus is on sketching, but everything that comes through within that initial five seconds after you express the trigger needs to go down on that paper. If you feel there is more coming in after five seconds, write down what you perceived during that first flush, then break contact by standing up and moving around, refocus, write that same trigger again, and sketch and describe what pops into your head during the five-second span. Do this until you intuitively feel that the information is complete. Breaking contact and retriggering will help keep the interpretive process of the analytical mind away from the information coming in. When you first break contact, you should get up and move briefly. Once you learn what it feels like to have the connection interrupted, you can remain seated. The contact ritual needs to be done only once a session. You do not need to repeat it after a short break in contact.

## Change of Perspective: Movement

Having the spirit contact change perspective slightly will help you obtain more information about the primary perceptions. Establishing a connection with the spirit is important before you start to work on a change of perspective. This connection should be made with the contact ritual before the session starts. Once that connection is made, you deepen it by working through the first primary perceptions. Do not make a big deal out of changing perspectives. By the time you do the contact ritual and finish channeling the initial primary perceptions, you will have an adequate connection to the spirit contact to change things around a bit.

Keep steady and work smoothly as you change perspective with your contact. If you are focusing on the session and the primary perception, you should not get any unusual sensations with this. Body sensations are only a form of mental processing that is being played out in the mind. They are related to expectation bias and should be ignored. The first way to change perspective is to ask the spirit to move around the primary perception. You can do this with any primary perception, even though it may not be a physical object. Moving around a concept involves studying an idea from a slightly different point of view. It is a little tricky to understand how moving around a concept is possible. However, movement and space are physical ideas that are symbolic in the Nexus. So this movement is a symbolic way of studying the concept or idea from a slightly different point of view. The idea is to focus with the spirit on moving around, going below, and flying above the primary perception, then triggering for additional data on those perceptions once you have changed position.

The change of perspective is symbolized by that moving around. To do this, I will introduce another trigger word, and that is the word *go*. The "go" trigger is placed in front of the main trigger, which is the "describe" statement. So, to move to the right of an object, you would write as the trigger "Go right and describe this object."

It is important when you do this that you know which object you want the spirit to look at with you. To help keep the primary perceptions straight and organized, I number the primary perceptions revealed in a session. If I have three objects, then I write "object 1," "object 2," and "object 3." That way, I keep all the objects that I perceived in the spirit's communication organized, so I can refer back to them and gain more detail through things like movement. I can go back to object 1 and do the move trigger.

Let's say, for example, that I want to change perspective and look at object 1 on my short list of three objects. I would write or say the trigger "Go right and describe object 1." My response will be the first thing that comes to mind—a sketch preferably, and a written description to go along with that sketch. I can go in any direction to take a look at this object with the spirit.

## Change of Perspective: Manipulation

A change of perspective can also be done by manipulation of the primary perception. This means you basically poke, prod, and play with the perception to elicit additional information. There are a couple of rules you have to follow here. For the trigger, you need to pick a word that is in the imperative form and is a verb (a part of speech that describes an action). Second, you have to do this for a primary perception that you already picked up in the session. That means you have to go back to what you have already written down, pick one of the primary perceptions, and work with it until you are satisfied with the information.

Here are some suggestions for the manipulation triggers: you can "touch," "smell," "lick," "squeeze," "tap," "throw," "enter," "leave," "stretch," "poke," "stroke," "kick," "roll," "fly," "toss," and "drop." I generally use "tap" and "touch." To employ the trigger, you write the imperative manipulation first, then ask for a descriptive response to the manipulation. Going back to our three imaginary objects (object 1, object 2, and object 3), let's say you want to manipulate object 2. You could write as a trigger, "Touch object 2 and describe what happens when we do that." The "we" is you and the spirit contact. Remember, the two of you are connected. You are working with the contact to gain more information about object 2. Once you finish sketching and writing down that description, you can continue to manipulate the primary perception (in this example, object 2) or you can move on.

In the next chapter I will go over how to use a spirit communication board for single-word and yes-no clarifications. Automatic sketching and writing should be your primary technique. The spirit board and dowsing are great tools for quick clarifications but do not work well for the bulk of the channeling session.

CHAPTER SEVEN

# DOWSING AND
# THE SPIRIT BOARD

Dowsing and the instrument known as the spirit communication board are tools used to clarify questions that come up during automatic writing sessions. In this chapter we will look at two basic methods of dowsing and then move on to the use of the spirit board.

Dowsing is a complex and multifaceted method of divination that can be used for very technical work once you develop the skills. It is discussed in some detail in *The Art of Scrying and Dowsing*. However, dowsing for clarification of the automatic writing session is relatively simple and easy to learn. It is used to find the answers to questions that have only two possible outcomes. Dowsing does not enable sketching. Sketches are more accurate, as a rule, for conveying information during channeling, and because of this I prefer to teach dowsing as a clarification technique rather than a primary channeling skill.

Dowsing is used after the main inquiry has been drawn randomly from the grab bag and you have completed your automatic writing session. The inquiry continues to remain hidden while you are dowsing. The focus of the dowsing will be on the primary perceptions that you unpacked during automatic writing. Triggers will also be used for dowsing. There are slightly different requirements for dowsing triggers than for automatic writing triggers.

## Dowsing Triggers

When you create a trigger for dowsing, your wording must be precise and clear, just as it must be for any other trigger. It also must be focused on the primary perception that you are trying to clarify. The dowsing trigger should not be focused directly on the hidden question drawn from the grab bag.

As with automatic writing triggers, the word *describe* is almost always used as the first word of a dowsing trigger. You can also change perspective, move, and manipulate with dowsing just as you can with automatic writing. The same rules apply for changing perspective. In the trigger, you use the words "go," "touch," "push," "poke," and so on, depending on the type of movement or manipulation you want to do.

If you do change the perspective, you should do it during automatic writing first, because the responses to changes of perspective are usually not limited to two possibilities. Dowsing should be done as a clarification. There may be situations where you need to change perspective to make the clarification, and the clarification meets the requirement of being limited to two possible outcomes. In such a case, you can move and manipulate when dowsing.

When writing a dowsing trigger, after the initial word "describe," add the phrase "through dowsing." This clearly indicates how the information is going to be perceived. You can make this even more specific by stating the type of dowsing you will be doing. Write down "through dot matrix dowsing" or "through pendulum dowsing" to make it even more precise.

For example, a dot matrix dowsing trigger to clarify the size of an object that was perceived during the earlier automatic writing session would be written like this: "Describe through dot matrix dowsing if this object is larger or smaller than a baseball." This trigger meets the requirements of being focused on the primary perception of *object*. It is a clarification of the automatic writing session, which unpacked the particular object in question. For the sake of the example, we will imagine there was a prior automatic writing session to go with this trigger for dowsing. The clarification trigger has two possible outcomes: the object is either larger or smaller than a baseball.

As you can see, the dowsing trigger is basically formatted in the same way as an automatic writing trigger. The same rules regarding leading statements, label seeking, and objective wording apply to dowsing triggers.

## Use of Comparative Dimensions

Comparing the primary perception object that you perceive to a second known object in order to determine its size will not cause a problem with expectation or belief bias. What's more, comparative sizing is a good tool to use with dowsing. You can use familiar objects for size comparisons because you are not trying to identify the primary perception of the object. Referring to our example, you are only comparing the primary perception object's size to a baseball. It is when you try to label the primary perception by asking "Is this object a baseball?" that you can get into the mindset that will lead to interpretive errors. This is label seeking and is detrimental to session accuracy.

The use of size or weight comparisons in a channeling session works better for most people than numerical measures such as inches or pounds do. Numbers tend to be more prone to expectation bias and are more difficult to work with than dimensional comparisons. This technique will help you find the size, weight, speed, and other details of objects perceived during the automatic writing session.

## The "No" Response in Dowsing

Dowsing works best when there are only two possible outcomes. If the outcome is not one of the two responses, there are ways to tell during dowsing that this is the case. It is called the *"no" response.* Having a "no" response as a third possibility is useful when channeling because it gives the spirit contact a way to cue you if there is something wrong with the trigger. It works as a fail-safe. I have incorporated the "no" response into the techniques presented in this chapter.

## The Need for Speed

Due to the mechanics involved in dowsing, it takes longer than the ideal five-second window to perceive a response to a trigger. Because the process is slower than is ideal for interpreting information from the spirit contact, I generally dowse with the responses hidden from my awareness. In dot matrix dowsing, the dowsing process itself does this automatically. Focusing on the primary perceptions and using dowsing as a clarification tool will help prevent the interpretive processing of your analytical mind from causing persistent inaccuracies. It is a bit more difficult to dowse accurately than to do automatic writing accurately. To help prevent analytical interpretation, start to dowse immediately after you ask the trigger question and work briskly.

## Dot Matrix Dowsing

This form of dowsing was originally based on dice-rolling divination. When I studied dice rolling, I found it to be less accurate than other methods of divination. Dice rolling relies on synchronicities to give you an appropriate response. I came to the conclusion that the deeper mind needs to play an active role and must have a way to influence the outcome of the divination. In other words, divination works best if the method can be controlled by the subconscious mind instead of by fate or synchronicity. I devised a method that uses dots but is also controllable by the deeper mind of the dowser. The result is the dot matrix method.

## Dot Matrix Technique

This section describes the dot matrix dowsing technique step by step.

1. To begin dot matrix dowsing, draw a square on a piece of paper and divide it into four smaller squares (figure 7.1).
2. Write your trigger statement next to the large square, making sure the wording is precise, short, to the point, and related to one of the primary perceptions.
3. Take a pencil and begin to tap its point on the paper so that a fair number of random dots fall into each quadrant of the square. Do the tapping briskly and without counting the number of dots. Focus your mind on the trigger as you tap. Make sure all the quarters of the square have dots in them. I find that a pencil works better than a pen for this purpose.
4. Once you finish tapping dots in all four quarters of the square, count the dots in each sub-square to determine the dowsing response.
5. If the number of dots in a square is even, then the response is positive. That means such things as "larger," a "yes" response, or "faster." It indicates positive gain. If the number of dots in a square is odd, then the answer is "smaller," a "no" response, or "slower." It represents a negative loss.

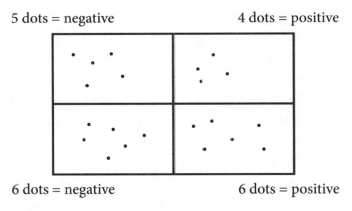

Figure 7.1

## Counting the Dots

There are two ways to tally the number of dots.

In the first method, you count all the dots in all four sub-squares to achieve a grand total. If the number is even, then the answer to the question is positive; if the number is odd, the answer is negative.

The second method, which I prefer, is to count the dots in each sub-square, then write the number of dots next to that quadrant. As with the first method, an even number is a positive or "yes" response to the question, and an odd number is a negative or "no" response to the question.

If you have three sub-squares with an even number of dots, it indicates a positive response. The answer is something like "greater," "heavier," "higher," or "faster," depending on the wording of the trigger. If you have three sub-squares with an odd number of dots, indicating a negative response, then the answer is negative, something like "lesser," "lighter," "lower," or "slower." If you have two sub-squares with an even number of dots, indicating a positive response, and two sub-squares with an odd number, indicating a negative response, then the overall outcome is a "no" response. The "no" response usually means there is something wrong with the wording of the trigger, or that it cannot be answered with just a positive-negative answer. This second method gives the spirit contact a chance to indicate something other than a yes-no response.

## Troubleshooting a "No" Response

When you have a "no" response, I recommend that you try rewording the trigger. Usually that will clear up the problem. The second way to troubleshoot is to look for signs of belief and expectation biases in the automatic writing session. If you are mentally interpreting information coming from the spirit, it will show up as inaccuracies in the automatic writing session, and the spirit is trying to point this out to you with the "no" response. A third possibility is that the spirit cannot determine the answer to your trigger in a yes-no format. The fourth possibility is that you became distracted and were not well focused during the dowsing. That happens with beginners who cannot yet tell if they are working with the spirit or are missing the channeling signal as it is coming up the thread. This situation will improve with practice and experience.

## Pendulum Dowsing

The method of pendulum dowsing that I use myself and teach to others is a bit different from what I have seen others teach. I feel that observation of the pendulum's movement is more accurate than trying to force it into a particular motion. In trained responses, which is the traditional method of pendulum dowsing, the dowser asks the pendulum to show a "yes" response by a predetermined motion and a "no" response by a different predetermined motion. If the pendulum does not move in the expected way, then the dowser deliberately and consciously sets the pendulum into that motion. By doing this, the dowser "trains" the pendulum to respond a certain way. Once the pendulum moves according to this intention, it is used for dowsing. This is how I learned to dowse years ago.

The second method of pendulum dowsing is to observe how the pendulum responds, rather than trying to make it do a certain movement according to the subconscious signal line. The pendulum response is due to the subconscious manipulation of a subtle natural muscle tremor that everyone has. The subconscious can control this natural trembling of the muscles of the hand and arm to some degree, and it is this tremor that gives the dowser the answer to the inquiry. In the observation method, you watch and learn what that response is. Your physical response is amplified by the pendulum and observed for changes. Through observation, you develop a line of communication using that inherent muscle tremor as a sort of code.

The best way to make the connection between the deeper mind and the pendulum is to simply watch it. There will be subtle changes in how the pendulum moves or trembles in the hand when the response is asked for. Learning the natural movements for "yes" and for "no" is the key to accurate pendulum dowsing. If you train the pendulum to respond a certain way, you are controlling it consciously, using the part of your mind that you are trying to exclude during a channeling session. This will cause inaccuracies due to belief and expectation biases.

To learn how the pendulum responds in a natural way in your hand, take a sheet of paper and write the words *yes* and *no* at least six inches apart. The pendulum should be on a string or thread and not a chain. The thinner the string, the better. Also, the lighter the pendulum, the better. I use a sewing or darning needle. A darning needle is a needle used in knitting that is around two inches in length. It is not as sharp as a sewing needle. I also like to use wood pendulums. I prefer lighter materials for divination because you have a hard time feeling the weight of the pendulum in your hand. Because of this, it is more difficult to influence or interfere with the movement. It is only when I am teaching that I will use a larger metal pendulum, because it is easier to see. If you really like a heavier pendulum, you can train to use it over time. It is, however, easier to start with a very light pendulum that you cannot feel when you are holding it. For a beginner, the darning needle is the best way to go. It is also very traditional.

Hold the string about four inches away from the pendulum and extend it over both the *yes* and the *no* on the paper. Say out loud "this means yes" as you move the pendulum over the *yes* on the paper, and say "this means no" as you move the pendulum over the *no*, and observe its motions. However the pendulum moves when held over *yes* or *no* is how your deeper mind will influence your body to respond with these answers. Do not influence the motion of the pendulum yourself by deliberately trying to make it move in a circle or do anything else. If the pendulum just trembles a little, that is what you need to watch for.

All you are looking for is a change in the way the pendulum trembles or moves. The differences between "yes" and "no" will be quite subtle most of the time. Whenever connecting to the deeper mind, what is subtle and gentle takes precedence over what is loud and dramatic. A subtle response is the best indicator of that gossamer thread connecting you to the spirit contact.

## Hiding Pendulum Responses

Hiding pendulum responses is another way to add a layer of protection against interpretive processing of channeled information. You may want to mark the possible responses ("yes" or "no," "larger" or "smaller," "heavier" or "lighter," and so on) on index cards, and then dowse with the writing of the responses facedown, so you see only blank cards in front of you. If you are working with a dowsing chart, I recommend covering the chart with a cloth and using a straight pin, which pierces the cloth and pinpoints the response on the dowsing chart. All you see when dowsing is the opaque cloth that covers the chart. If you are dowsing with a covered chart, you will only see the "yes" response in the pendulum. It will indicate where you need to stick your straight pin to mark the response, which will be revealed when you uncover the chart.

Hiding responses in this way can be a good remedy if you are having trouble with dowsing accuracy. In very technical dowsing, such as with topographical maps (maps used in orienteering and navigation), I always hide the map. I usually make a series of blank sheets of paper that represent sections of the map. I cover all this in greater detail in *The Art of Scrying and Dowsing*, if you are interested in learning more about dowsing.

## Spirit Board

The spirit board was my first introduction to spirit communication, as I related in my book *Spiritual Alchemy*. Essentially, a spirit board is similar to a dowsing chart. The traditional spirit board has the letters of the alphabet arranged in two crescent rows (like a double rainbow) across the board, with *Yes* at the top-right of the board, *No* at the top-left, and *Goodbye* centered near the bottom. *Maybe* and *Maybe Not* are sometimes written in the lower left and right corners of the board as well. The popular name for such boards is the Ouija board, but spirit communication boards in their various forms are much older than the commercial product sold by Parker Brothers for so many years.

Traditionally, a spirit board is operated by two or more people who rest their fingers on an inverted shot glass or on a triangular piece of wood with three legs that is usually known as a planchette. The planchette is moved intentionally in loose circles for a few seconds at the start of the session, then begins to move seemingly by itself in response to questions. It stops intuitively on a letter, the letter is recorded, and the channeled message is pieced together letter by letter and word by word in this way.

This presents a problem for the solitary practitioner, since at least two people are needed to operate a planchette effectively and a third person to record the results. It is quite hard to do all this by yourself. In order to accommodate solitary practitioners, I use the pendulum technique and treat the spirit board as a dowsing chart. You do not need a Ouija board for this. The best materials for the communication board are paper and cloth. Cloth is better. The letters can be painted on the cloth in any order. The *Yes, No, Goodbye, Maybe,* and *Maybe Not* can also be painted on if you wish. I use a second cloth to cover the letters when I am dowsing the spirit board, so that all I see is a plain cloth. I use straight pins (the kind you use in sewing) to mark the areas that the pendulum indicates should be marked.

You will need the following items to make your spirit board:

- White cloth, preferably duck canvas (the kind you use for oil painting)
- White acrylic paint for a primer
- Black paint for the letters
- A paintbrush
- A pendulum with a string (A darning needle works well for this.)
- A second opaque cloth for a cover (should be the same size as the board)

Prime the cloth that serves as the spirit board with white paint, and let it dry on a flat surface. I suggest using two to three coats of white paint, depending on the quality of acrylic paint you are using. I do not recommend using oil paint for this, since lamp-black color oil paint takes a month or more to dry completely. On the back side of the cloth, put some white paint or glue to prevent unraveling. If you know how to hem the edges, do the hems and glue down the loose threads along the edges.

Use a pencil to sketch out the letters on the dried white paint on the face of the cloth. The letters of the alphabet need to be well spaced in the shape of a double rainbow across the board, with *Yes* and *No* at the top corners of the board and *Goodbye* centered at the bottom. The words *Maybe* and *Maybe Not* can be added to the bottom corners if there is enough space. Paint the letters in jet black or a deep blue color. It is not necessary to paint on the numbers from 0 to 9 that appear on commercial Ouija boards. No numbers should be used on your board. The process of dowsing numbers is usually not very accurate and should be avoided. I suspect that numerals work in the same way that labels do, and are a result of mental processing rather than true perception.

Trim your opaque cover cloth so it is the same size as the spirit board. It is best to leave the cloth plain, without any ornamentation, since this can be a distraction. You can hem the edges of the cloth if you wish. Have your pendulum on its string, along with six or eight straight pins, and you are ready to go.

Unlike when using other dowsing charts, covering and disorienting the letter cloth is optional. Disorientation is sometimes used in chart work that involves dowsing. (Refer to my book *The Art of Scrying and Dowsing* for more information on the use of disorientation.) Generally, once you cover a pendulum chart, you disorient it with the cloth on top by rotating it randomly so you do not know where the responses are under the cloth. When you are channeling, the inquiry is hidden, so it is not necessary to disorient the chart in this way. It is, however, a good idea to cover the letter chart with an opaque cloth to provide the channeled information with additional protection from belief and expectation biases.

## Triggers for the Spirit Board

The triggers for the spirit board are the same as for a dowsing session. The way you learn information through the spirit board is just a specialized form of dowsing. The triggers follow the same rules and technique. This includes the rules about focusing on the primary perception that you are trying to clarify, keeping the questions objective, and avoiding label seeking and leading questions. The difference between the triggers for the spirit board and the ones you use for automatic writing is that the spirit board triggers should be answerable in one to two words. The spirit board is a tool for clarification of descriptions and primary perceptions that you unpacked from the automatic writing session. Ideally you should not use it for the bulk of the channeling session. The spirit board is far too slow, and you cannot get the accuracy and detail that you can get with the automatic writing technique I presented. The spirit board does not allow for sketching, so it will always tend to be less accurate.

## Using the Spirit Board

Dowsing for a response on the spirit board should start right after you write down the trigger. To do the dowsing, pass the pendulum over the cover cloth very slowly until you have a positive response. When you get a positive response, stick a straight pin through both layers of cloth. Continue dowsing and marking the places indicated by the spirit with a pin. Work without looking at the board until you have several pin marks. When you have a number of pins in place and intuitively sense that the spirit has finished, carefully roll up the cover cloth from the bottom to the top to expose one pin at a time. Find the letter closest to each of the pins you placed. Write down the letters as you uncover them. If two pins fall on a single letter, write that letter down twice. If a pin falls on a word, and the word answers the question, then you should examine the individual letters to see if there is any additional clarification to the one-word answer. If there is no clarification, then the letters can be disregarded or additional questions can be asked.

The word formed by the individual letters is going to be like an anagram. The letters will not be in order. The word may not be spelled correctly. When you intuitively feel that you have completed the session, look at the letters and see if you can piece the puzzle together. The spirit contact will often give you out-of-order words and abbreviations to help you avoid biases while you are working with the spirit board. This is why I recommend that you piece the puzzle together after you have selected the letters. This helps you avoid the traps of the mind.

If you cannot figure out what the clarification is, then you can rephrase the trigger and try again. The spirit board is not a particularly easy tool to use, so be patient with it. With a bit of practice, this technique will give more consistent and reliable results than traditional Ouija board methods do, and it can be used by the solitary practitioner.

# CHAPTER EIGHT

# TRANCE CHANNELING: BASICS

In this chapter I will discuss the basics of *trance channeling*, a traditional form of channeling that adds a couple positive aspects to spirit contact interaction. It can help open the door to experiences with nonphysical entities other than basic exchanges of information. It allows the channeler to have a richer, more fulfilling personal experience than merely sitting at a table and writing. Anyone who channels spirits or other entities, either alone or as part of a group, will benefit from trance channeling.

My trance induction technique has changed a fair bit over the years. The changes are the result of experience and experimentation. I went over this topic in my first book, *Spiritual Alchemy*, as it was taught to me by the spirits I was working with at that time. That was over ten years ago. I do not mean to suggest that the presentation of trance channeling in *Spiritual Alchemy* is invalid. It is both practical and workable. The techniques I teach today and describe in this book represent the evolution and improvement of the techniques I practiced a decade ago.

Though trance channeling does offer some interesting experiences, the emphasis should always be on the accurate communication of information from the spirit contact to the individual or group. Trance is the last step of the channeling session structure that I have been outlining in this book.

## Definition of Trance Channeling

Trance channeling is when the channeler goes into an altered state of consciousness and communicates with a spirit contact. The trance state can best be described as physical relaxation coupled with an alert and focused mind. It is a normal daily occurrence, part of your everyday sleep cycle. It also occurs when you are bored or drowsy. Trance channeling is communication via channeling in that relaxed state. The focus of the mind goes inward and decreases physical sensation and awareness of the physical body.

During the trance state, the spirit contact is drawn to the channeler through the use of the contact ritual—the same ritual that is described in chapter 4. The main difference between trance channeling and the basic contact ritual is that trance channeling intentionally moves the mental awareness away from the physical body. For trance channeling, the contact ritual is done more slowly, over thirty minutes or so. Mentally, the awareness is more focused on the steps of the contact ritual than on the physical environment. This way of focusing for a short period of time will naturally create a trance state.

## Increased Intensity

Trance channeling creates a change in the experience of channeling that differs from the experience of automatic writing and other techniques that I have described in previous chapters. Writing while sitting at a table is not particularly exciting. Trance channeling offers a deeper experience that increases subjective perceptions, such as the sense of presence of the spirit contact. It may facilitate clairaudience, clairvoyance, visions, and different sensations of the body. While these things do not increase or decrease the accuracy of channeled information, they make the channeling experience more exciting and interesting. Trance channeling ramps up the energy level of the encounter, which is beneficial to both the spirit and the channeler. Intensity helps in connecting with a contact and is also desirable for spiritual growth and insight development.

## Physical Manifestations

Spirit contacts and nonlocal primary telepathic entities must use a physically based channeler in order to create physical manifestations. In most spirit contact circles, one of the primary goals is to see these manifestations, so let's go over what they are and examine some ideas as to why they happen and how. As you develop channeling skills and begin to do trance channeling, you may find that physical manifestations are occurring.

Physical manifestations are anomalous events that are directly or indirectly influenced by the spirit. They can occur spontaneously and sometimes unpredictably. Paranormal manifestations include movement of objects, the appearance of lights, spirit apparitions, sounds that have no obvious physical origin, mists, and temperature changes in the air. They can also include anomalous visions and sensations. These are considered to be supernatural manifestations when they are witnessed by more than one person, and indirect manifestations if the channeler is alone.

Indirect manifestations can take the form of synchronicities that have the appearance of luck or chance, changes in life goals, and alterations in the behavior of people or animals that depend on the focus of the spirit entity. Some of these indirect manifestations can be perceived through the five physical senses, while others are internally based and subjective in nature. They are valid indications of spirit activity, even though the nature of an indirect manifestation is usually a subjective personal experience.

## Manifestation of Presence

The sense of a spirit's presence is one such subjective manifestation that will intensify with the use of trance channeling. You can tell if a spirit is present by the feel of the room or other location where the channeling takes place. This is what I call *affective atmosphere*. It is a subtle change on an emotional level. Animals are very sensitive to this and will sometimes react with curiosity, or fearfully if they are not accustomed to it. The sense of this manifestation is a feeling that someone unseen is watching that someone is present in the room. Sometimes you get a prickly sensation, particularly in your head and arms.

Manifestation of presence is difficult to describe in physical terms. Most people just say that they felt the spirit's presence. This indicates a detection using subtle senses. A sense of presence may be caused by slight changes in temperature or air pressure; changes in the Nexus that we do not yet even have terms for; things that we cannot readily see, such as ultraviolet or infrared light; or low-frequency sounds that cannot be heard but create subtle vibrations that can be detected through touch. When I use the term *subtle*, I mean changes that are hard to pinpoint and describe.

Often a spirit's intention, friendliness, and willingness to communicate are also present with this sense of presence. It is probably the most important manifestation to learn to detect when working with deeper channeling and manifestation circles. Manifestation circles are groups of people who attempt to create the conditions necessary for paranormal manifestations to occur. Physical mediumship groups and human-initiated extraterrestrial (HiET) contact groups are examples of paranormal manifestation groups.

## Trance Channeling Accuracy

Working with trance channeling may or may not affect the accuracy of channeled information. The channeler's mind is alert and active during trance. The mental processing still functions in the same way as when the channeler is awake. The issues with belief and expectation biases are still relevant when trance channeling. However, the focus of the channeler is more inward during trance, and because of this you may find that the trance channeling information is more accurate than what you get in pen and paper sessions. As the focus moves progressively inward, the mind begins to passively perceive without analyzing more than it does in the normal waking state. This is a subtle change and varies from channeler to channeler. The result can be an increase in accuracy and a reduction of bias, depending on the degree to which the mind is focused on observation and able to maintain its passivity while in trance.

Exclusion by hiding the inquiry is a technique that is more consistent than trance, and works as a powerful tool for increasing accuracy of channeling sessions. Trance is not as consistent as exclusion, but it is helpful for some people. If you use the two techniques together, you can have a powerful and accurate channeling session.

The session structure with hidden inquiries and the grab bag technique should be practiced even when trance channeling to avoid problems with accuracy. In the channeling system set forth in this book, I have included trance channeling as part of the overall channeling session. Trance is not a stable mental state, especially at first. Because of the activity of the conscious mind, even in a deep trance, there are still the same basic risks of imposing mental beliefs and expectations on the channel as you are working. The trance sessions will be less accurate if they do not have a specific focus or if the channeler knows what the focus of the session is supposed to be while channeling. In the first case, lack of an explicit inquiry allows the mind to run wild; in the second case, conscious awareness of the inquiry tends to introduce beliefs and expectations.

The accuracy of trance channeling can improve with experience. However, even with an experienced and very talented deep-trance channeler, I have observed problems with belief and expectation biases. Edgar Cayce is one example. He did not always have an accurate on-target session even though he used deep trance states.[7] Cayce was a very talented psychic who could attain an extremely deep trance that had better than average stability and consistency. If someone as incredibly gifted as Cayce could not be completely accurate, then what can be done? Can we have a more accurate session than Cayce using the setup for channeling outlined in this book? The answer is yes, we can, because we know things now about how channeling works that we did not know a hundred years ago.

I believe the best solution to the problem of accuracy with trance channeling is the same one I presented earlier in the book that addresses accuracy in channeling in normal waking consciousness: hide the subject of inquiry, use a structured session, and study the feedback. These three keys are vital to accuracy no matter which channeling technique you use, or even if you use one that I am not covering in this book. Channeling accuracy can be attained with any type of channeling technique. With these three keys in your possession, you need only learn the technique and you will be able to work accurately. Going back to Edgar Cayce, he was able to compensate for his biases because he had a naturally passive, visually oriented, well-focused mind. There is every chance that you and anyone else who uses the keys I have given in this book will be able to channel just as accurately, or even more so, than the legendary prophets of the past. It is a matter of skill, technique, and practice—nothing more is needed.

---

7. See William A. McGarey, *The Oil That Heals: A Physician's Successes With Castor Oil Treatments* (Virginia Beach, VA: A.R.E. Press, 1993), 11; and Jess Stearn, *Edgar Cayce: The Sleeping Prophet* (New York: Bantam Books, 1971), 13.

I will go over a few aspects of trance channeling that people may have questions about. I do not have the level of natural talent as Edgar Cayce. I do, however, have a fair bit of experience, and I practice constantly. The experience of trance channeling is varied, but the goal of the channeler should always be to relay information that is accurate and true to the actual communication of the channeled entity. Whether the channeler is working alone or in a group, the focus is best kept on communication. The rest will fall in place as it is needed. If physical manifestations happen to occur, look upon them as a bonus.

## Unusual Sensations in Trance

Trance channeling can be accompanied by some really weird sensations. If you are aware that this is the case before you begin, then you will be less nervous about feeling odd things. Sensations vary from one session to the next and from one person to the next. I do not recommend seeking out these sensations. They tend to happen when they happen and are not usually predictable. The focus of channeling is *always* accurate communication. That is the experience you should be after.

Tingles, heat, cold, dizziness, and a rapid or slowed heart rate can all be felt during trance channeling at different times. Sexual arousal can also sometimes occur. If that happens, it should be ignored. Shifting your focus to physical sensations in your body will break your trance. I usually experience hot flashes, which are unpleasant, to say the least. I can end up completely drenched in sweat after a trance channeling session. I also have weird mental sensations of being in a different "space." Initially when I experienced that particular sensation, I would worry about losing my body, and break trance. Eventually I became accustomed to the odd sensations and learned to move on, pretty much ignoring them.

These odd sensations might bother you for a while until you get used to them. They can be startling at times and cause you to break your trance. Just keep at it and you will eventually relax and learn to ignore the weird buzzes, sounds, sights, and other nuisances that distract you from the task at hand. It probably took me a year or two before I was comfortable with these strange sensations.

Sometimes I find it comforting to have music or soft ambient sounds playing in the background that I can use to help my focus. There is quite a bit of meditation music available out there. Anything that is not too busy or distracting is okay to listen to. None of these odd sensations has ever caused me anything more than a startle. No harm has ever come. Contrary to my initial concern, I have not lost my body, and when I come out of trance, I usually take a nap and then have dinner. I do not believe there is any inherent danger in trance channeling.

## Practice for Resilience

You have to practice handling distractions to make your trance resilient and stable. Developing resiliency in trance training is necessary if you want to work with a group. Going to a public place and sitting surrounded by other people while you induce a trance is a good way to develop resistance to distractions. Working with annoying ambient noises, such as traffic sounds, loud music, or people moving and talking, is also helpful in developing a resilient trance. Once you learn how to do trance channeling, you should go out and practice the trance induction in different locations to help you learn to keep the trance stable for the period of time required regardless of what is going on in the environment.

## Trance Session

When you want to do a trance channeling session, you start by doing an automatic writing/sketching session as described in the previous chapters. This gives you some sketches and information to work with in the trance channeling session. It makes the trance session more focused and easier to do.

When I say that trance channeling is an extension of the normal channeling session, I do not mean that it must be done over a long period of time. In fact, I recommend that you generally keep the total channeling session under an hour. You will develop issues with deterioration of focus after about forty-five minutes, even as an advanced practitioner. You can practice multiple sessions in a day if you need to do detailed or extensive sessions. You can also do the paper and pencil session one day and work with trance channeling the next.

As long as you do not reveal what you drew out of the grab bag, you can work on a single question over several days and multiple sessions if you want to. The subject of inquiry will continue to remain hidden from the conscious mind of the practitioner during the trance sessions. You do not reveal the grab bag contents until all channeling is completed.

## Triggers for Trance Channeling

After the paper and pencil channeling session is completed, you will then have a trigger for trance channeling. It should only be one imperative statement if you are working alone. The trance-channeling trigger will relate to the entire previously written session. The focus is still on the primary perceptions. You will continue to elicit descriptions instead of seeking labels or making guesses. Images, movement, and emotional and sensory information (information relating to the physical senses) will continue to be the priority and focus. Trance session triggers should be along the lines of these examples:

- "Describe the most important aspects of these primary perceptions."
- "Describe any message you have regarding this session."
- "Describe additional information or corrections regarding the channeled information received in this session."

The trigger is written down and uttered out loud at the end of the pen and paper work, just before initiating trance. This inquiry allows the spirit contact to make any corrections or additions to the information you have already perceived. The response you perceive in a trance channeling session is subject to feedback and reality checks in the same way as any other channeled perception. The spirit contact should stay focused on the topic. I find that allowing this time in trance for additions and corrections often provides the best information of the channeling session. You should work on obtaining additional data about information that has already been unpacked in the automatic writing session. As with dowsing and the spirit board, trance channeling is a tool for clarification and for increasing the detail of the information perceived during the written session.

## Recording the Trance Channeling Session

It is helpful to work with a partner who can observe your trance state and speak the triggers to you when you are in trance and focused on the spirit contact. The partner can then write down the responses of the spirit, which you speak aloud. If you want to do a more complex trance channeling session on your own, you can use a digital voice recorder that you turn on when you start going into trance.

If you do not have someone to work with and are not using a recorder, you can try to remember the information you received while in trance. In this situation, the response of the spirit to the trigger has to be short enough for you to retain the information as you return to normal waking consciousness. Transcription of the voice recording from the session should be in the form of sketches as much as possible. It is important to sketch the responses immediately after the session or you will forget them.

During the trance session you will be talking out loud, either to a voice recorder, to yourself, or to someone who is writing down your perceptions during the trance. When I first learned to do channeling, Edward Kelley taught me to say out loud what I was perceiving, even though I was working by myself. Talking out loud gives your mind a toehold in physical reality and helps reduce loss of information while in trance. It is especially helpful for those who tend to drift into sleep when trance channeling.

## Summary of Key Points for Trance Channeling

These are the key points in setting up a trance channeling session.

1. The automatic writing session should be done prior to initiating trance.

2. The goal of the session remains hidden when doing trance work. The inquiry pulled from the grab bag is not revealed. The purpose of the trance channeling session is to clarify the information received in the automatic writing session.

3. Practice trance channeling in less than ideal places that are noisy and have distractions present in order to develop resiliency.

4. Use trance-channeling triggers that are worded to relate to the paper and pencil session just completed.

5. Use a voice recorder to record your trance sessions. Get into the habit of describing your perceptions as you move into and through the trance-channeling process. If you work with a partner, both of you should be trained in channeling techniques. Transcription of the recording should be done as sketches as much as possible.

# CHAPTER NINE

# TRANCE CHANNELING: METHOD

In this chapter I will take you through trance induction and trance channeling step by step. You do not have to be in an unusual or special state of mind to do trance channeling. It is a normal, everyday state of daydreaminess and relaxation, and just a little closer to sleep than full waking consciousness. Trance can be very deep or superficial. With this technique I am not looking at full trance mediumship. The depth of trance you achieve develops naturally when you have good channeling focus.

Do not overcomplicate the induction of trance. Trance is induced in a sitting position, with the feet on the floor the back supported, and the head free. Your bladder needs to be empty. If you have trouble with hip or knee pain in the sitting position, you can do this lying down, but you will likely nod off into sleep at times. Dozing is harmless, but when you nod off during trance channeling, it means you will need to start the trance over again when you wake up. Sometimes trance is harder to induce just after you have taken a nap. Sitting up helps prevent falling asleep, as your head will drop down when you doze off.

I will go over two methods of trance induction. They are basically the same as the contact ritual. The first trance induction method relies more on the intuition of the channeler than on visualizing specific imagery. The second method uses elemental imagery in a similar way to the elemental contact ritual in chapter 4, and has a bit more detail for those who want something specific to focus on. One method is not a more advanced version of the other. I have included two methods due to the differing needs of readers.

To induce a trance, you close your eyes and relax, focusing on naturally tense areas of the body, such as the muscles around the eyes, jaw, shoulders, and back. Breathe deliberately at a slow rate. With each exhalation, allow yourself to slide down deeper within. Follow each breath deeper toward sleep without actually going to sleep. Once you are focused and relaxed, you can establish your safe talking place. You can do this in four to five deep, slow breaths. As you learn the skill, you can work with deepening the trance if you want to. This is done by slowing the mind and increasing physical relaxation as you open more to the spirit contact. A passive sense of listening and following the spirit contact will create the desired effect.

## The Safe Place

The goal of the initial phase of trance induction is to be very relaxed and calm in your body and fairly alert in your mind. It is the same basic process you use when you go to sleep, but you stop before you fall asleep. Once you are settled and relaxed, with controlled breathing and mental focus, you create in your imagination a nice, comfortable safe place to meet the spirit. You want to imagine a scenario where you meet the spirit to sit and talk. The key to doing this correctly is to feel safe and focused on communication without danger or distraction. The specific imagery you use to create this affective atmosphere is not nearly as important as the feeling that you have established focus and safety.

For visually oriented channelers, an imaginary garden, a wood grove, the beach, a camp site, or a room in a house would all work fine. Keep the imagery of the safe space simple, with the focus being on the spirit contact and the communication taking place. This "location" is where you are going to talk to the spirit contact. It needs to be consistently imagined, regardless of whether you are focused more on visual imagery or on emotional feelings of safety and privacy.

When you enter trance, the first thing you will do in your imagination is create this safe place. It is not a bad idea to practice doing this a few times before moving on to the second part of the procedure. Trance will happen naturally if you are involved and focused on the affective atmosphere of the safe place while sitting comfortably with your eyes closed. The proper mental state will happen without doing anything deliberate to make it occur. Trance is the natural result of a change of focus from the outside world to the inner mind.

The exact content of the safe talking location is not as important as the feeling of security. Once you have established this place with an entity, it is helpful to keep the imagery the same in subsequent meetings with all spirits that you do channeling with. Developing specific communication paths and consistent patterns helps to improve accuracy and makes channeling easier under less than ideal conditions.

Predictability and safety with a mental channeling setting are helpful when communicating with entities that have strong emotional needs related to safety and consistency when working with a channeler. Many nonhuman intelligences have a greater need for predictability than humans do. Animal spirits are an example of a class of entities that has a need for consistency, safety, and predictability. Some accounts of extraterrestrial contact experiences that I have read over the years, particularly in *Onboard UFO Encounters* by Preston Dennett, indicate to me that these extraterrestrial intelligences also have a significant need for predictability and safety when dealing with human beings.

For instance, if you like the idea of a picnic bench at a favorite park, you need to keep that setting in your mind as the place where you will talk to the entity on each subsequent occasion. The whole effect of the setting imagery is sort of like a daydream. It can be reinforced with photos, drawings, or even models if you are so inclined. This kind of reinforcement is a bit overkill for a basic channeling session. It becomes more important when you start to add elements of setting or are working in a group and need to be consistent with how other people are focusing and imagining the safe place.

You do not have to hold every visual detail of your safe place in your head while you talk to the entity. It is sufficient at the beginning of the session to establish in your mind that this is the location where you will be meeting. The sense of imagining the safe place is no different from holding a familiar destination in mind while you drive to it. You do not hold an intense visual image of your destination in your head while you are driving; instead, you develop the idea that it is where you want to go, and then you get in the car and drive there.

The purpose of the safe place is to feel secure while you are interacting with the entity, to have a predictable setting where conversations happen, to create a pathway to allow you to go into trance quickly and easily, and to make your trance state more resilient so you can work in more distracting physical locations.

## Linking the Safe Place to a Physical Location

The visualized safe place needs to be associated with a physical location in your imagination. This is the same physical location where you are holding your channeling session. However, sometimes the physical location may change. If you are working with a group or you want to visit a place and try an experiment, then you will be changing your physical location—I am talking here about the channeler's location. You need to get into the practice of creating a link between the physical location where you are working and the mental interview location in your imagination where you interact with the spirit. The link is created by making the safe place merge with the physical location so that the affective atmosphere of the physical location is the same as that of the safe place. You are not trying to imagine changing the appearance of the physical location to look like another place. The emotive feeling of the safe place is what is superimposed over the physical location.

Some places are easier to do this with than others. If there is a location that is known for supernatural sightings or occult phenomena, that is often a good place to hold a channeling session. If you do not know of any place with supernatural associations that is convenient to get to, then just work with what you have. If it is a room or an apartment, that is fine. To create the link between it and the safe place, superimpose the mental location over where you are located physically.

It is also helpful to know what your physical location looks like from the air directly above it. Satellite images are useful for this. Study these images and incorporate them into your contact ritual. I am not sure why this works, but having this aerial view in your imagination significantly increases the sense of presence of the spirit contact. If you feel it does not work for you, then try an alternative method and view the place from a chthonic perspective by mentally going deep beneath the earth and rising to the surface. If you are working with a group, have prints of the imagery so everyone is focusing the same way at the same time. If you cannot hold the images in your head, then work from emotive feeling rather than visual imagery. Aids in visualization are given to help you. If they do not work for you, do not get upset. Work with your mind, not against it.

## Rising Through the Planes

Once you have your safe place in mind and also mental imagery of the physical location from high above or from beneath it, then you can start casting a line to find the spirit contact. You guide the entity from its location in the Nexus to your location on Earth. What you will do with this ritual is create a visually or emotionally based scenario that makes it easy to reach out and guide the entity in. The scenario exists only in your mind—it is imaginary. When you pay attention to creating this focus and physically relax toward sleep, you will naturally go into a trance.

## First Trance Induction Ritual

With this trance induction method, you focus on and feel your mind rising slowly away from the earth. You imagine that you are ascending through layers or planes. This is similar to the contact ritual, but you are doing this in a deeper way and in a more relaxed state of mind. With each plane that you pass through, you use your breath to silently chant an open vowel sound, such as *Oooooh* or *Aaaaah,* to help you stay focused on the plane. Keep your throat open while you do this. Allow your jaw to drop open naturally so that you can stay very relaxed with this chant. Do not tense up your jaw.

The chant is done silently with the exhalation of breath. You do not need to use your vocal cords. You can use actual vowel sounds or words vocalized aloud if you want to, but I think it is best to focus more within rather than outwardly on physical reality. If a group is working together, you may need to start out actually vocalizing the *Oooooh* or *Aaaaah* chant and then move on to a silent chant once the rhythm is established. The idea of silent vocalization is to keep your mind poised between sleep and waking, and focused on moving upward through the etheric planes. It also serves to slow and deepen your breathing. Opening your mouth for these silent vowels makes your jaw more relaxed. We tend to hold tension in our faces.

Each plane you ascend through has a higher and more intense spiritual energy and less physical energy. The Nexus is connected to all planets in this universe and to all universes. It is the in-between place: a hallway, so to speak, with an infinite number of doors; the world between the worlds.

As you rise through the planes, you can observe in your imagination a transition from a deep blue-violet color to a pure white light. Allow these colors to naturally change and lighten as you ascend through the Nexus. While you are doing this, reach out to the spirit contact. Do not worry about visualizing specific colors in specific places; just start with violet-blue and make it become lighter. You cannot let your mind focus too much on physical things, such as color changes, or you will not be able to find your spirit contact, which is the purpose of the induction. Just let your mind create what is best for you. Trust your intuition.

You do not have to know the name of the being you are calling to you—just reach out and mentally feel for it. As you cast out with your mind, you mostly look for a sense of presence or a sense of touching. By the time you are doing this, you will have already made contact with the entity in the paper and pencil session. All you are doing is reestablishing and deepening the connection that you made earlier.

It is important that you learn to feel for a spirit contact, rather than relying on the spirit's name, its appearance during life, or other physical aspects. This intuitive reaching for a sense of presence is how nonphysical entities identify each other. It is also a more universal form of identification between species. The name or other symbolic identifier is used when you do the pencil and paper session, but when you trance-channel, you are looking for the more intuitive feeling of presence that will have developed by the time you have completed the initial contact ritual and the pencil and paper channeling session.

With each breath, you cast your awareness further afield and rise higher above the earth. The physical satellite imagery is a good aid to help you feel this viscerally. However, you do not look at the images when you are performing the actual trance ritual, but just when you are learning how to do it. Trance should be worked with the eyes closed and the mind focused. You cannot look at photos while inducing trance.

Once your are in "orbit" above the earth and you have risen in your mind until the light is clear and white, start to reach out and feel for the spirit contact. There are no physical markers or symptoms that indicate when you are ready to call the entity. You need to go by how you feel, and trust that your intuition will guide you to where you need to be, mentally, in order to do this effectively.

Do not fuss over picky details of imagery. If you imagine things a bit differently as you rise through the Nexus planes, such as different colors, that is not a problem. It does not necessarily mean anything, other than being an indication of how your mind is working at that moment. The only thing you need to worry about is keeping your final goal in mind: you are drawing an entity down to a safe place where you can interact with it. Try to keep focused on that as your goal, and do not allow your mind to wander around too much. If you can picture the imaginary place clearly, that's great, but if you go more by feel than visuals, that is also fine. In presenting this imagery sequence, I am merely trying to give you an idea of what should be happening in your mind and what it will feel like. The end result is that the entity is guided to the safe place to talk and interact with you.

Do not worry about how the trance feels or if you are in a trance. If you worry about the trance itself, your nose will start to itch or you will suddenly feel a need to pee. Trance does not work well if your attention is on your physical body. Focus on the task you are accomplishing, not on how you feel.

Be patient with the entity's response. It may take a bit of time for the being to perceive you and figure out what is going on, even if you have just been in an automatic writing session with it. This is a different level of connection you are making with the spirit contact than in automatic writing. The connection may not happen instantly for the spirit. I find that it usually takes from five minutes to about half an hour. I can hold a trance for about forty-five minutes, so if I do not get a response from the entity in a half hour or so, I end the session and take a break.

When a connection is not made, most of the time the issue is not the spirit contact but the channeler. The entity has already communicated with you in the previous channel-tuning and topic-based session. You may not be focusing, or there may be distractions that you cannot ignore. Resetting your mind and body by taking a break will usually resolve the issues with focus. All you do is keep the inquiry that was drawn from the grab bag hidden in a safe place, change your activity for a time, then go back to trance channeling when you return. If you take a break from a session, you do not have to repeat the automatic writing prior to doing trance.

It does not matter how much time has passed since the paper session. If you have completed a paper session, you can do trance channeling on that session any time after, as long as you have not revealed the topic of the inquiry. It will not make any difference if it is a week, a month, or a year later. You simply pick up the session where you last stopped. However, if desired, you can review the perceptions from the automatic writing session just to remind yourself of what you need to seek information about in the trance session and to regain your focus on that particular inquiry.

The entity's response will be experienced as a sense of presence. The feeling of presence will vary quite a bit from one trance session to another. At times it can be overwhelming and freakishly powerful, yet at other times with the same spirit the contact may be barely detectable. Accept what you perceive. The initial automatic writing part of the channeling session is really helpful as a way to make contact, because by the time that is finished, the entity will have perceived you and focused on your presence. The automatic writing session creates a fairly light contact with the entity. As we deepen the focus through the steps of the trance-channeling technique, there is more of a manifesting presence felt.

## Guiding to the Safe Place

Once you feel you have made contact with the entity, return the way you came, down through the Nexus planes, descending very slowly back to the physical location where you are working. Do this with the imagery of lowering gently to Earth, as if you were flying a glider and going down through the clouds while seeing the location where you are actually located. Take breaths that are gentle and slow. Ease down into the place where you are sitting, and guide the entity into the superimposed safe interview place. Look for that subtle sense of presence. If you are working with others, they will feel it as well.

## Interaction

The third part of trance channeling is the interaction with the entity. You have selected one of the three trigger statements listed at the end of the preceding chapter. Wait for the entity's sense of presence to develop at your location before you proceed to work with the trigger and interact with the entity. It is important that you gently focus on that sense of presence. Do not try to grab it or hold hard to it. Being tightly held is unpleasant for a spirit contact. Just try to relax and open to what the spirit is expressing to you. Keep your mind quiet and still. The feeling of that state of mind is similar to listening intently for a faint sound.

Having that sense of stillness when the contact's presence begins to become perceivable is really important to hearing the spirit and channeling accurately. That stillness needs to be maintained throughout the session. The most difficult part of channeling, I find, is allowing the contact to be close to you without grabbing or holding on to it. When I first started developing clairaudience, it was very natural to be rather grabby because I was afraid I would lose the channel. I had to learn to adjust my focus so that I was not either grabbing roughly and holding on, or letting go and not perceiving anything. You do not have to be clairaudient in order to learn to adjust your focus and intensity. This applies to working with automatic sketching and writing as well. Most of the spirit contacts who are familiar with humans are aware that this is something that has to be learned, and are patient with it.

Be friendly, project a wordless welcoming feeling toward the spirit, and provide a quiet, distraction-free mental landscape. The image you have of the entity is not important. The sense of its presence is. Once that is established, the entity is present with you in the space you have created. When the entity responds to your invitation, speak the trigger directive you wish to present to it out loud, and repeat aloud the response you perceive from the spirit exactly as the entity transmits it to you. You can use a digital audio recorder or have an assistant write down a record of the session on paper.

Do not interpret what the entity says, but merely repeat its words exactly as you perceive them. Use descriptive language, remembering that it will have to be transcribed as sketches. Focusing on images and descriptions of those images in your telepathic communication and recording will help both you and your contact stay on track and reduce intrusive biases.

When working alone, it is best not to present more than one trigger directive. The trance state you have achieved will develop instability if you channel for too long. If you are working with another person, that person can speak a series of triggers for you to transmit, one by one, to the spirit, and can record your narrations of the spirit's responses to them. The other person can also guide you through trance and help you to maintain it with verbal suggestions. The second person should watch for signs of trance instability, which usually manifests in the form of restlessness, changes in breathing pattern, or loss of focus. When that happens, the assistant should guide the channeler out of trance, and the team should take a break.

During trance, you will generally talk more slowly than when you are in a normal conscious state. Talking out loud needs to become habitual in trance. Even if you are alone, you should practice this as part of your normal routine. I found it difficult at first to maintain a good, solid trance and talk at the same time, but it does get easier with practice. If you are working with someone else, you should agree on a signal for the other person to start recording information. Raising a finger is a good signal that can be done without breaking the trance state.

## Elemental Trance Induction Ritual

This is the second trance induction method. The main difference between the two methods is in the detail of the imagery. You choose which induction method works best for you. The additional detail in the elemental version may help keep you more focused. This helps as you deepen the trance. The idea you are visualizing of ascending through the elements, moving out and above the earth, is not to be taken as a literal representation of the nature or location of the spirit contact. Instead, it is a step-by-step mental distancing from the physical world and moving toward the Nexus, which is connected to everything. It is important to have that mental distancing take place. This elemental ritual is one example of how to accomplish that. The focus away from the physical and on the Nexus is the most important concept presented in this ritual format.

You can label the layers of ascent and the etheric planes in different ways. You may wish to use more or fewer layers in your ascent. They can be related to such things as the chakras of the human body, or the spheres on the Tree of Life, as the Golden Dawn's Rising on the Planes ritual does. There are lots of different symbolically meaningful sets of concepts you can use. It is fun to play around with the symbolic imagery and see what works and what does not. Always remember that the end goal of this ritual is for the entity to be in the safe talking place and interacting with you there.

### Earth

The first layer of ascent is related to the earth element. The colors are dark. The darkness represents physical density. The quality is physical and earthly. You want to feel this as you rise through the dense layers of the physical world.

### Water

Think of water vapor that is like fog or rain. The color for that would be a blue or green. It will be lighter in tone than the earth colors and lights. Because we are ascending through the elements, the water concept should be more like rain and fog than a terrestrially bound body of water.

### Air

As you rise higher, the element of water gives way to the element of air. It is dry and cold, with a feeling of clarity and purity, similar to the experience of breathing the air on top of a high mountain. The element of air has a feeling of clear open space. The air element in this visualization also includes the area just above the atmosphere of Earth. The colors are transitioning to a lighter yellow tone. The colors do not have to be exact. The idea is that they will become lighter as you rise.

### Fire

In this layer you reach Earth's "orbital space," where the light is bright and clear. The element associated with it is fire. The sun is the predominant feature. In space, the sun has less color and is more of a clear, hot light. It is also a concept of purity. Space is more sterile than the surface of the earth. Any organisms that survive in space are small, light, and able to withstand the fierce solar radiation and extreme cold of outer space.

### Spirit

You finally transition into the element of spirit. The light is a pure white light. You deepen your connection to the source of life and spirit itself, with its many beings, intelligences, and emanations. It is the source of all beauty and love. You can now make contact with the entity you desire to speak to.

## Homing Beacon for the Spirit Contact

Once you reach the level of the Nexus, you reach out with your mind and touch the entity gently. When you feel a sense of the spirit's presence, simply reverse what you did above, descending through the elemental layers back to the physical world. Draw the contact to your safe location, dropping down to Earth as if you were flying down from orbit.

It will take a few times through the trance channeling session to learn how the process works and get it memorized. Do not worry about knowing whether or not you have attained trance. Relax and focus on the progressive imagery and feel of the ritual. You will need to have this book handy and refer to it during your first few sessions. As you memorize the steps, you will find your natural trance state if you focus on the process and goal rather than on how you feel. That being said, trance basically feels like you are daydreaming in a really boring class at school or a meeting at work, when you are focused on something in your imagination and lost in that imaginary setting.

The ideas for trance induction given here are just a way of helping you get into that place. The general procedure is to rise up, find the entity, and guide the entity back to the imaginary safe place you have superimposed over your physical location. As you do so, you will develop a sense of how each step feels, and then you can just work by feel rather than imagining every step. The guiding of the spirit down to a safe location superimposed over your physical location has to be kept intact. For trance channeling, this is your anchor. The sequence you are using should be memorized. This is why I have made the trance ritual resemble the contact ritual—to help you learn and remember the sequence.

## Transition to a Manifestation Session

In some channeling styles, trance sessions lead to attempts to produce paranormal manifestations. If you want to do a manifestation session after channeling, do it after both the automatic writing session and the inquiry for the trance channeling are completed. I will write a few brief words about this kind of channeling.

Start the manifestation session by directing the entity to give you a sign of its presence. Do this by means of an imperative statement. When you state this trigger, you will notice that the entity will come closer to you. The sense of its presence will increase, and things will become more focused. You may feel as though you are in a slightly different "space." This difference is hard to describe. There is an increased sense of intimacy, and your body may feel different. The idea is to focus more within, keeping quiet and still, with a receptive mental state. It is a peaceful experience, but can feel a bit weird sometimes.

Continue to state the trigger for the manifestation as your intuition directs. I personally do this if my attention starts to wander or I have random thoughts intruding on my focus. Stating the trigger helps to keep the mind sharply focused, which helps the spirit channel the energy for the manifestation through you. Usually you can work in this way for a half hour or so before you lose focus and become fatigued. At that point, whether or not a manifestation has occurred, it is time to end the session. This is a process that requires an energetic buildup. That buildup is handled on the spirit contact's end. I mention it only because it has been consistently observed that manifestation work does not usually succeed right away. You do not do anything to build up the energy except be open to letting the spirit do things that might feel strange while maintaining a steady, calm trance. The other factor is to practice frequently and to communicate with the spirit about how to improve your channeling.

Producing paranormal manifestations works better with a group than with an individual. Everyone in the group must work in unison for the common purpose and be fully and equally focused in their intention. Even then, you will find that inducing manifestations takes both time and skill and is not predictable. Not all the conditions needed for a paranormal manifestation to occur are known. There are environmental factors as well as psycho-spiritual factors involved. Such things as wind, rain, temperature, humidity, and air pressure may play a part. On the other hand, channeling to seek knowledge is easier to do for a single person, and is more fulfilling and less frustrating, especially for a beginner.

## Releasing the Entity

The final step in the trance session is releasing the entity. As the entity moves further away from you at the end of the session, consciously release the entity, then shift your awareness to greater alertness and the normal waking mental state. It is important to distract your mind after you let go of the entity, so that the entity will not have a residual binding to you once the communication work is done. Residual binding can be a nuisance and might interfere with your sleep or your subsequent communications with other entities, should you desire to do another session soon after. It will fade fairly quickly on its own, but it is a good habit to release the spirit contact's connection and energy by engaging in physical activity once the communication is finished. If you desire to incorporate a ritual into the basic channeling session, the releasing of the spirit contact is done through a benediction and formal dismissal. The ritual itself is not effective without the visceral feeling of removing your focus from the entity back to physical life. Once you complete this, you should not be thinking about or trying to sense the entity's presence. The feel of what the ritual is trying to do is more important than the wording, and is what makes the dismissal effective.

To remove your focus from the session, quickly sketch the spirit's responses to your inquiry, then get up and do something physical to distract your thoughts. Physical activities such as eating or walking are the best way to do this. Once you feel the session is cleared from your mind, transcribe in a more formal way the spirit's answers that you hastily jotted down so that you will be able to easily read them in the future, or write down the verbal material you narrated into the voice recorder.

## Summary of the Trance Channeling Technique

Two trance channeling methods (elemental and rising through the planes) are described in this chapter. This is a summary of the key points of the techniques presented.

1. Select a spectrum of inquiries for the grab bag that relate to the topic you hope to learn more about from the spirit contact. For beginners, stick with human spirits and terrestrial animal spirits whose lives have a large number of historically verifiable detail. Place a minimum of four inquiries in the grab bag. Draw one out and set it aside without looking at what is written on the paper.

2. The automatic writing session is next. Normal waking consciousness is maintained for the first part of the session. This session is done with pencil and paper, sitting at a table. In group practice, all members of the group participate in channeling.

3. The trance-channeling trigger is selected from the list provided at the end of the preceding chapter. Trance-channeling triggers allow the spirit contact to make additions and corrections to the perceptions that were written down during the automatic writing session. Triggers need to be answerable in descriptive terms and must not lead the spirit to say what the channeler expects or believes.

4. A safe interaction place is created using the channeler's imagination. It needs to be used consistently when interacting with spirit contacts. This imaginary safe location is superimposed over the physical location. The channeler should be able to imagine the physical location from above, as if flying over it in a plane.

5. Trance is induced and the safe location is briefly held in the mind while in trance. The channeler then imagines slowly rising above the earth as the trance deepens. The imaginary color of light goes from a deep violet-blue to pure white. The focus is on the spirit contact and not the body of the channeler. Sensations should be ignored.

6. Contact with the entity is done from "orbit," or when the light from ascending the planes turns a clear white. When the entity returns contact by giving a sense of presence, the channeler guides the entity down to the physical location, using visualization of the appropriate satellite imagery, and into the mentally created safe place for interaction.

7. Interaction with the entity takes place and is recorded by speaking aloud into a recorder or to an assistant who writes the information down. After the interaction ends, the entity is released and the channeler deliberately changes focus and activity to ensure that no residual contact with the entity remains. If you are doing a formal ritual, you can close according to the directions of your particular ritual.

8. The slip of paper is opened and the inquiry revealed. The information from both the written session and the trance session is compared to known physical details. This is the feedback session. Beginner feedback sessions need to have inquiries with details that are historically verifiable, as this will enhance the channeler's accuracy.

# CHAPTER TEN

# A CASE STUDY IN SESSION ANALYSIS: EDWARD KELLEY

W hen you channel, the channeling session itself is done with exclusion—that is, hiding the target inquiry. *Analysis* is the part of the session where you reveal the inquiry to yourself and work with the raw session
data in an effort to understand the communication that came from the spirit
contact. Analysis allows you to see where you have experienced intrusive biases
and what you perceived correctly through channeling. This is the part of the
session where you put the whole story together. Looking at the raw session data
as a whole, you will not be able to see how it fits the question right away. You
have to study the session data against the revealed inquiry, looking at what you
wrote, perception by perception, to understand what you saw. You need to do
this without forcing the data to fit your preconceptions. It is a balancing act.

*Feedback* consists of assessing the mistakes made during channeling and
trying to understand the causes of those mistakes. Studying your errors will
help you improve your focus and accuracy as a channeler. To learn about yourself, your beliefs and thought patterns, is to learn how to become accurate at
channeling.

Analysis and feedback need to be done without fear and without desire.
The best way to explain how to do them is to show you with the example of
an actual channeling session, explaining as I go through the data how I fit the

pieces together to gain useful and accurate information. The channeling session in this chapter is one I did with Edward Kelley, in which I practiced exclusion and used the basic session structure outlined in the earlier chapters of this book. The raw data is found in the illustrations that follow. They show what I wrote during the session before revealing to myself the inquiry drawn from the grab bag.

I will go over each step of the procedure so that you can understand how the session fits together and flows. As I go through the data, I analyze the information perceived during the session and do feedback to examine the validity of that data.

## The Spirit Contact

I do not expect everyone to accept without question the claim that I am talking to the alchemist Edward Kelley during this session. All I can say is that I have seen, heard, and interacted with a contact who claims to be the spirit of this man.

Edward Kelley (1555–1597) was a gifted seer. He was born in northern England and spent some time studying law at Oxford University before dropping out without obtaining a degree. It is questionable whether he practiced law legally, and he may have been involved in coining (counterfeiting) at some point in his early life. Edward Kelley was especially renowned for his scrying ability. He met Dr. John Dee in 1582 and started working as a professional channeler and scryer for Dr. Dee. He died trying to escape from a prison in Bohemia, a kingdom of Europe that was located where the Czech Republic is today.

My history with Edward goes back to 2011, when I learned to use a radio to channel spirits. Edward instructed me in channeling and helped me learn to scry, among other things. The history of the initial channeling experiments from 2011 to 2012 was recorded and published in my first book, *Spiritual Alchemy*. Since that time I have continued to have a relationship with this spirit contact, and because he is partly responsible for this book as well as *The Art of Scrying and Dowsing*, he gets to do the case study for us today.

The first thing I did for this case study was to make a series of grab bag questions. The first question in the list in the next section is a good calibration question, as Dr. Dee wrote in some detail on that particular day (March

10, 1582) about his first scrying session with Edward. Since I have historical documentation on hand related to Dee and Kelley and their work together, I composed several questions that have verifiable aspects based on that information. I did not include a channeling improvement question in this grab bag, as I wanted to demonstrate how historical information can be enhanced using the channeling techniques presented in this book.

## Grab Bag Questions

These are the inquiries I put into the grab bag for the session on Dr. John Dee and Edward Kelley. The date referred to is from the diaries of John Dee. The book referred to is an edition of the original diaries written by Dr. Dee found in the Sloane Manuscripts in the British Museum.[8]

1. What happened during your meeting with Dr. John Dee on the Saturday of March 10, 1582?
2. What did the main house of Dr. John Dee's Mortlake estate look, sound, and feel like?
3. What did the atmosphere, Dr. John Dee, and others present look, sound, and feel like during your first meeting with Dr. John Dee?
4. What did the equipment associated with your alchemical work look, feel, and smell like?

A question was drawn from the grab bag and set aside. I did not observe which question was taken until after the sessions were completed. This case study was done in two sessions. There were actually two separate grab bag draws for this case study. I drew the same question for both sessions. I decided to combine the sessions for this case study instead of working with two different questions. I placed all four questions in the grab bag for both drawings.

Even though the grab bag contents were not revealed until after the session was done, I will reveal what it was here. This will help you, as a channeler, to understand what the raw session information looks like and how it relates to the question. The question drawn was number four: "What did the equipment

---

8. See Joseph H. Peterson, *John Dee's Five Books of Mystery: Original Sourcebook of Enochian Magic* (Boston, MA: Weiser Books, 2003), 66.

associated with your alchemical work look, feel, and smell like?" Edward, in his channeling, expanded his response to include the immediate surroundings. I included "smell" in the question because, during my initial channeling sessions with Edward in 2010, he had mentioned that the homunculus had a nasty odor associated with it. I think odor is an important factor to ascertain when trying to discover what is present and what is going on at a location.

After I made the grab bag draw and put the question aside, I conducted with Edward Kelley the short contact ritual described in chapter 4. I can connect easily and nearly instantly with him since I have channeled him quite a bit over the past ten years.

## Channeling Session One

Once the connection with Edward Kelley was made, I focused on the primary perceptions and intuitively felt that there were three: *object, presence,* and *activity.* These perceptions were felt and written quickly.

The image at the top of figure 10.1 describes an activity that was associated with Edward's alchemy: traveling. This image came to me first but did not relate to the initial primary perception of *object.* Any time this happens, you should still sketch what comes to you. The sticks are probably rows of trees, and after the session I felt that this was likely a snapshot of the road going to Mortlake. The traveler, represented by the stick figure, is Edward. He cuts across a field to go where he wants to go. The trees or sticks line the road. I felt that this was likely the case because the entire setting in the channeling session had the feel of being very early in the employment of Edward with Dr. Dee.

When doing feedback, the first image that came to me should be considered a miss, even though it is likely something that really happened. It is a miss because it is off-focus. It is not related to the question or the first primary perception. I got an associated label with this traveling of "Oxford." In this case, I simply left the label as it was, set it aside, and did not break it down. I did not feel that it was related to the session's goal. This was an intuitive move on my part. Expanding a label is always a judgment call. There are times when I sense I am not quite on target and tend to leave what I have put down and move on to other perceptions.

**Figure 10.1**

There is another possibility that the data relates to obtaining alchemical supplies. There may have been traveling involved to obtain materials, or the sketch may relate to the story of Edward finding the red powder of alchemy at Glastonbury Tor and going off the path to secure the stash. Without perceptions to clarify this image, the data is too incomplete to be considered valid or helpful. If I were to go back to this session in the future, I would request a clarification of that image in the list of grab bag entries. The amount of clarification needed for this first ideogram is too extensive to work through using dowsing or the spirit communication board. It required an additional channeling session.

The second image on the right with lettering in the box is related to *object*. There is foreign writing. I cannot exactly place the writing. It is in a foreign language, and not one that I am familiar with. Most of the manuscripts and books that Dr. Dee had were not in English. The object is associated with alchemy, so it is probably one of those books or manuscripts. I get a label of "Greek." I feel this label is symbolic of the idea of being a language and writing system that is unknown to me. Letters may be imperfect when seen through scrying or channeling. Orientation may be reflected or inverted. The expansion of the label "Greek" is "foreign language, unknown writing system, does not feel familiar, feels exotic and foreign. The spirit contact feels curious about it."

I will note that the period of time that this session seems to cover was very early in Edward Kelley and Dr. Dee's relationship. For this reason, I do not think it is the Enochian alphabet scryed by Kelley. It does appear to be a single time period that Edward was channeling. He did not appear to jump to different points of time. Edward's emotive response was curiosity, which means he did not know what the object was and wanted to find out.

The second primary perception is *presence*. In the image to the left of the foreign letters is a figure that is described as "male," "thick," "black," "cloth like," "scratchy," and "heavy." Dr. Dee was a tall, thin man. I get the impression that this is probably Edward himself. He seemed to be a smaller but heavier man than Dr. John Dee. The black cloth-like covering is probably a cloak for warmth. It is coarse, scratchy, and heavy, with a very dense felt-like texture. It should be of interest to note that earlier in his life, Edward was pilloried and allegedly had his ears "cropped" (the ends cut off) for coining, after which he was said to always wear a cap to cover his ears. Yet in this image, if indeed it is of Edward, he is bareheaded. It could be that both he and Dr. Dee wore the same sort of cloak, and in that case, unless they were side by side, we would not be able to identify who is who. The cloaked figure could also be a third party, perhaps the person who introduced Edward Kelley to Dr. Dee. Even though I feel it was Edward Kelley, it is important to take a look at other alternatives. Belief and expectation biases can still be inserted into the interpretation after the session. When you do session analysis, you do not have the shield provided by exclusion.

The third primary perception is *activity*. The activity was focused on a wheel-shaped object that turned up in both channeling sessions. In this session, it was the wheel shape that was associated with an emotive response of a happy feeling, a sense of good fortune, the lifting of a heavy weight. In the post-session analysis, I feel that this wheel shape relates somehow to the alchemical furnace. In looking at images of alchemy furnaces, I found several that had wheel-shaped tops. The spoked wheel was perceived by looking top-down at the furnace, I believe.

The second channeling session was clearer in this regard, as the object was too hot to touch and had an orange fire-like glow when looking down into it. I only had an outline of the image in the first session. It was the center of the activity. In the second session I picked up more detail, and this enabled me to figure out what Edward was showing me and how he felt about it.

In the background and the surroundings, it felt cold, cloudy, and hazy. Edward thought he'd had a turn of good luck. His emotions felt happy, fortunate, and relieved. It seemed as though his prayers had been answered. He saw Dr. Dee as amazing and intelligent. His thoughts were, "Wow, this is for certain a real alchemist." *Presence* is closely tied to the objects and activity that were presented as the focus of the session. I think overall the channeling information is useful and adds to the knowledge of the known historical facts.

Another image came to me in the foreground, and that is the sketch in the bottom-right corner of figure 10.1. It shows the words "table like" next to the image of a figure, which is next to a table. This is a primary perception of *object*, with an accompanying ideogram. The table-like structure was artificial and had several smaller objects on it that were taller than they were wide. The second primary perception in the ideogram is *presence*. This is a male figure behind the table, who had something white on his head. I cannot be sure if this was a covering or natural hair that was rather tangled. It was clearly light-colored and fitted his head closely. It is something that I am not familiar with. It almost looks like white dreadlocks. It was weird and unexpected, and I felt somewhat repulsed by it.

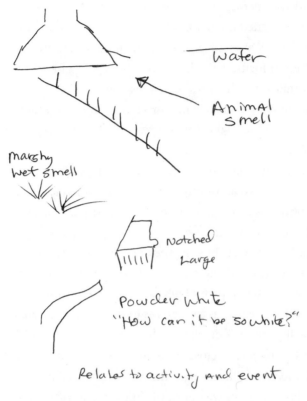

**Figure 10.2**

The next group of images is interesting (figure 10.2). I am not sure if the first image here is on focus or not. It appears to be in the background and involves large objects related to a location. The ideogram is an object, a large artificial structure that is not related to a structural object that people would live in.

A strong smell of animals was present. It is possible that the alchemical equipment was used in an outbuilding or yard. My interpretation is that Dr. Dee kept the alchemical supplies and equipment out of reach of his many children, friends, and relatives who frequented Mortlake. The shape of the roof of this building is rather squarish on top. I was able to find examples of this shape in thatched roofs in England by searching through images online. The barn and Dr. Dee's residence have not survived the centuries, so I cannot provide feedback on the accuracy of the image. However, it is in keeping with structures of his period that have survived, so I would say it is likely to be accurate. There is a marshy, textured landscape nearby and a body of water in the background. The odor of animals is strong. Transportation-related infrastructure is nearby.

For feedback, this data is interesting and, I think, relevant and reasonably well on focus. The location of alchemy experiments can be considered to be part of the equipment description asked for in the question.

I did a pendulum dowsing to clarify the size of the structure, and found that it was rather larger than a house, more the size of a church. The pendulum dowsing was done by hiding a plus sign and a minus sign. The tasking statement was "Describe the size of this object (structure). (+) means larger than my house and (−) means smaller than my house." The plus and minus signs were hidden during the dowsing. I also felt that the structure was big. I was rather surprised by the large size.

There was an object that is labeled "notched" and "large." I am not sure what to make of it. It appears to be a large building and part of the upper sketch. Because it is not clear, this would be considered a miss and off focus in feedback, and would lead to a request for clarification being placed into the grab bag in a later session.

The smaller object to the left, next to the words "powder white" and the question "How can it be so white?" relate to *activity* and an event. I believe the narrow-neck tubelike ideogram represents an alchemical retort. This is verifiable as a piece of equipment used in alchemy. The white powder is related to that sketch. The impression Edward gave me was a certain level of his surprise at the whiteness of the white powder. The white powder is one of the products of alchemy, and is also verifiable as part of the inquiry.

Triggers were done throughout the session. I have worked with Edward to the point where I just have to change mental focus and the images comes to me. In this case, it happened so fast that I did not have time to write down the trigger because I was trying to get the information down on paper quickly. It is possible to slow down the data coming in and write out the triggers as you go. I remembered to do this in the second session.

If I had not known this contact, or I was having trouble with the data being difficult to unpack, I would have asked for descriptions of the objects and the two presences. As you gain experience, you will find that the information comes very fast, especially if you are working with a spirit contact you know well. If the triggers had been written out during the session, they would have been "Describe object 1" and "Describe the first presence." I would have gone into describing presence one's purpose, focus, and activity. I would have seen the wheel and asked for the object's purpose, temperature, and texture, along with the sounds and surroundings at its location.

This concludes the data and analysis from session one. As you can see, there were additional primary perceptions uncovered during the session, as well as data that was incomplete and could stand to be explored further. This is always the case in a channeling session that is properly done. This basic information could very easily be expanded into thirty or more pages. At some point you have to make an arbitrary decision to stop.

My focus and accuracy improved as the channeling session progressed. This is an example of where the channeler's focus can affect the quality of the session. Edward channeled information in a compressed form that included information about the background buildings and other features that were present along with the alchemical equipment. As we continued to improve the connection, the data became more specific to alchemy. Honesty about the analysis and feedback will help improve focus.

## Channeling Session Two

The next channeling session was done the following morning. The same questions were put into the grab bag, and I drew number four a second time.

When I started the second channeling session, I first intuitively perceived four objects and a presence (figure 10.3). These perceptions happened quickly. They were detected and were written down within seconds. I felt that I should start with the second object, as it attracted my attention with its bright blue and red colors. The ideogram was flapping and cloth-like. It was covering something, and there was a snapping sound near it. I remembered to slow down the data stream and write out the triggers this time. The trigger was written "Describe the size of this object." The response was "as tall as a person, going wide and going tall." I then perceived the word "rich." I asked, "What do you mean by 'rich'?" The response was "colors, textures, artistic craftsmanship, special, valuable, attractive, beautiful."

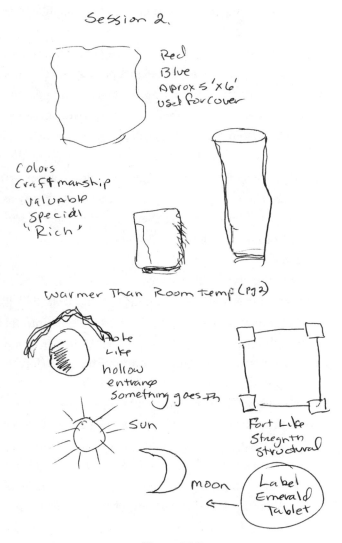

Session 2.

Red
Blue
Aprox 5' x 6'
Used for Cover

Colors
Craftmanship
Valuable
Special
"Rich"

Warmer Than Room temp (pg 2)

Hole
Like
hollow
entrance
Something goes Th

Sun

moon

Fort Like
Stregnth
Structural

Label
Emerald
Tablet

**Figure 10.3**

The next two sketches relate more specifically to alchemical equipment. The sketch of a tall object on the right feels like its purpose is to contain and hold something. It is hollow, round, not even, a bit irregular in its shape. It is opaque; it is not glass-like in texture or appearance but has a metallic feel to it. The sides are thick and make a dull sound when we tap on it. The smaller object beside it is made out of the same sort of material. There is something like smoke coming out of it and falling downward.

I perceive a label of "Emerald Tablet." This is a document that describes in poetic form the process of alchemy.[9] This label breaks down into symbolism present in this poem of the sun and moon, which represent gold and silver. In this case I see the ideogram of the symbolic alchemical sun and moon together, which I sketch at the bottom. Temperature dowsing was done on objects that were later revealed to be equipment used for alchemy, particularly the object that appeared to be a furnace. (In the sketch this is the oblong object with the arch over it.) The comparison was to room temperature. So the tasking was "Was this object (arch over the circle) warmer or cooler than room temperature?" I got a positive indication from the pendulum dowsing using the observation method I described in chapter 7.

In the middle is a hole-like, hollow object with some kind of covering over it. I do not think the covering is solid—it may be a cloth-like or leather-like texture. I write down next to it in abbreviated form, "Something goes into this." Next to that image, on the right, there is a square object that is similar in structure to a fort—strong, artificially made, and square, with some other reinforced structural components at the corners. The size of this object is unknown. I feel it is directly related to alchemy and could be part of the furniture involved in the work.

So far, this session seems to be directly related to alchemy. I have good focus and a good connection with Edward, who is providing me with quality snapshots of his experience with the alchemical experiments. It adds a few details that are historically likely but not directly verifiable. Even though the label "Emerald Tablet" is directly related to alchemy, it is still a label, and should be broken down into descriptive terms. Remember that while I was channeling, I was practicing exclusion. So I did not know if the Emerald Tablet related to the question drawn from the grab bag or not.

The ideograms of the symbolic sun and moon are how that statement broke down. The ideograms of the sun and moon are images that represent the goal of Dr. Dee and Edward's alchemy experiments. They describe in symbolic form

---

9. See Donald Tyson, *Three Books of Occult Philosophy Written by Henry Cornelius Agrippa.* (St. Paul MN: Llewellyn, 1993), 709.

the purpose of the equipment. The breakdown of a label into ideograms that are somewhat like a label, and in themselves need to be broken down, happens occasionally. The ideograms in this case summarize and symbolically represent the purpose and overall goals of the alchemy experiments, including the scrying sessions and angelic invocations. The angelic invocations and scrying sessions were attempts by Dee and Kelley to gain secret knowledge of how to successfully do alchemy, and because of this I included these in the symbology represented by the sun and moon ideograms.

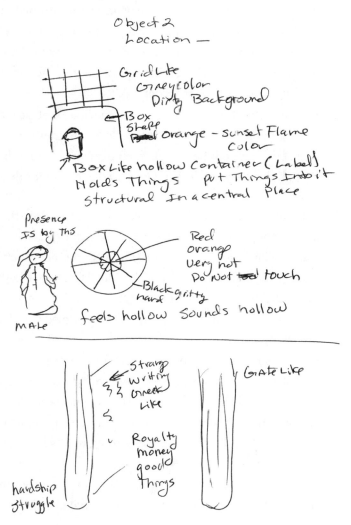

**Figure 10.4**

The sketch near the top of figure 10.4 is of object 2 and its location. It is a detailed and interesting perception. I am fairly sure, after analyzing it post-session, that it represents a fireplace where the alchemical experiments were done. There is a grid-like structure above the large boxlike object. The object itself is rather rounded in appearance, hard, grey in color, dirty, and sooty. A strong orange glow is present. The glow is obviously a fire that is burning within the large boxlike object. I describe it as "orange-sunset flame color." The general temperature in the room is rather cold, considering there is a fire burning there.

Inside the fireplace-like box is a boxlike structure with a domed top. This is not in the fire, but is next to it at the edge of the fireplace. A label of "homunculus" surfaces. I break down the label into relating to a structure in a central place, smelling of animal feces and rot, incorporated into life but also apart from it, and involving advanced psychokinetic skills.

The domed, boxlike structure matches some of the images of alchemical furnaces I found during research. However, this could be another piece of equipment. I cannot tell at this point. It does appear to be on target and well focused.

In session, it might have been helpful if I had tried to dowse for the measurements of the larger boxlike object that I interpret as a fireplace, and the smaller boxlike object that I interpret as alchemical equipment, possibly the furnace. Doing this measurement probably would have helped determine the purpose of the smaller container-like structure. This would be a good point for clarification in another channeling session, and could easily be added to the grab bag contents.

I also receive an affective response of fear of failure, resistance, and an overshadowing presence that is mildly threatening. This is coupled with intellectual problem solving, trying to figure it out, finding a solution. Fear is motivating the problem solving. A lot seems to be at stake here. The fear is very intense, almost demon-like. At this point, I move to a presence behind this and perceive the following: "This is wow, intellectual focus, lively, aging, absent-minded, religious, obsessive-compulsive." There is an associated presence of a young girl. Again, I see the same man with the funky white thing on his head. He is completely covered in a scratchy black material.

At this point, Edward shows me more detail of the wagon wheel structure. It is a tube-like structure that glows with a fire orange in the middle. It is metallic and hollow. It is too hot to touch. It is black and gritty, very dirty, and smells like hot metal.

For the final part of the channeling session, I trigger by saying, "Describe the most important aspects of the session." The response is the image at the bottom of figure 10.4, a gate-like ideogram with wall-like structures containing writing on their surfaces. I could not read the writing. I felt a longing to be inside that gate. Inside were associations such as "royalty," "money," and "good things." These ideograms are symbolic; they are not literal objects. Outside that gate was hardship and struggle. This gives the overall feel to the use of the alchemical equipment. The secret of alchemy meant a relief from struggle for Edward Kelley and Dr. Dee.

## Summing Up

This concludes the channeling sessions. I hope it gives you an idea of how the sessions flow, the focus on the primary perceptions, and how to break down labels. As you can see, there is data from the session that is interesting and useful in understanding the question, but there is also data that is off focus. This is typical of a channeling session using this method. Often a question is answered, but you end up with additional questions by the time you finish the analysis.

In these two channeling sessions, we learned a few new things about Dr. Dee and Edward Kelley. First, the alchemy was done either outside or in a barn-like structure away from the main house. The second is that Dr. Dee's alchemical furnace was round and probably on the small side for a furnace. I perceived some of the feelings and thoughts that Edward Kelley was experiencing through this work as he started his employment with Dr. Dee. I believe these sessions represented the time period when they were still at Mortlake, before they traveled to the European continent.

Each channeling session will be unique. Perhaps the most difficult part of a session is putting the pieces together with the question so you can gain an accurate picture of what you channeled. It requires some practice and experience, as well as objective judgment, to weave the pieces together. When you channel, you are perceiving snapshots. Like assembling a slideshow using separate photos, you stitch the images together to gain knowledge of the bigger picture.

Channeling is an art, and part of that art is weaving the pieces into a coherent overall picture. It has to be done objectively and with honesty.

As a beginner to this system, you need to use questions that can be validated through research. In this way, you will learn how your mind and your perception work. When you first look at your session data, you may not see the connection to the question. You have to take the information you perceived piece by piece, focusing on the primary perceptions, in order to weave the whole thing together. If you are not honest about what is accurate and what is not, about what is focused and what is not, you will see a deterioration of your skills and, subsequently, your accuracy.

If you do not have data that is related to the question, simply put the question back into the grab bag, take a break, and try again. Remember, you are not trying to guess which question you have taken out of the grab bag. Always focus your attention on the primary perceptions. Most problems in session are due to poorly written questions and triggers or to the channeler trying to guess the hidden session goal.

# CHAPTER ELEVEN
# A CASE STUDY IN
# SESSION ANALYSIS:
# EDGAR CAYCE

I have two more case studies to share that demonstrate the techniques and results that are interesting and reflect what a channeling session should look like.

All case studies for this book had to be written in such a way that you, the reader, could follow what I was doing at the time. In order to accomplish this, I had to write out more of the descriptions than I would have if I were working alone. Actual sessions mostly involve making sketches and then breaking down labels into descriptive terms beside the sketches. This is how a session should be done. In these examples, I add some descriptions that will help you understand the flow of the session. The idea is to create a feeling of being there during the session, so that you can see and feel what it is like to use the channeling technique.

This chapter will present a case study of a channeling of Edgar Cayce. Cayce was a man who lived in Kentucky and Virginia in the late nineteenth and early twentieth centuries. He developed a technique for diagnosing and treating medical problems through the use of self-hypnosis. He was very successful in doing this.

*Spirit contact:* Edgar Cayce, a historical figure
*Grab bag questions:* Partially verifiable; intermediate to
    advanced level

1-A. What are the etheric and energetic actions of herbs that cause an etheric as well as physical effect on the spiritual and physical environment and on beings?

1-B. What are the effects of herbs on the spiritual and physical levels, and how do those effects differ between fresh herbs, dried herbs, and essential oils of herbs?

2-A. How is nonphysical sensory input coming solely from the Nexus perceived and processed by a human being?

2-B. How do the physical, etheric, and environmental conditions, as well as Nexus conditions, affect the accuracy of this type of perception?

3-A. What are the etheric and energetic effects of stones, and how do they interface with the Nexus to create changes in the physical, energetic, or etheric environment?

3-B. What are the concepts underlying their most effective possible use for desirable and intended change?

4-A. How do the sun and other planets affect physical health and spiritual well-being, and how can their effects be best utilized?

4-B. What are the concepts underlying these conditions, and how can they be best sensed and utilized?

## Note on Grab Bag Questions

These grab bag questions are conceptual. The purpose of this session is to illustrate how well sketching works when doing conceptual inquiries. For a beginner, I would recommend also adding historical questions about Edgar Cayce's life. Mixing questions where there is good historical material to compare with the session helps prevent straying into bias. This session was feedbacked using my personal knowledge of the readings Cayce made during his life. I obtained this knowledge through a group called the Atlantic Fellowship Conference, which meets once a year. I have been participating in this group since about 2014.

## Session Interpretation

*Question 3 (parts A and B) reveal:* "What are the etheric and energetic effects of stones, and how do they interface with the Nexus to create changes in the physical, energetic, or etheric environment? What are the concepts underlying their most effective possible use for desirable and intended change?"

The contact ritual was done. The first trigger was "Describe the primary perceptions relevant to the hidden inquiry." In this text I have described my post-session interpretations for clarity. The question was not known to me at the time of the channeling, and the interpretations were added after the channeling was completed. When reading these descriptions, it is important to study the sketches, since the text is an expansion and explanation of the sketches.

I started the session by intuitively sensing the primary perceptions. I found three of them: *concept, presence,* and *object*.

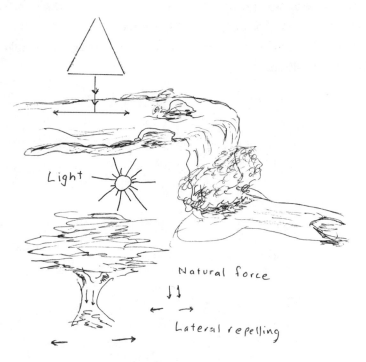

**Figure 11.1**

In the first sketch (figure 11.1), the equilateral triangle presented itself with an unspecified force going down and then laterally. This triangle was then placed in what seemed to be a river of etheric energies. Force was flowing down from the triangle into the symbolic river. The label of "river" was broken down into "flow, circulation, movement," which was clarified to indicate passive movement caused by natural force. Gravity appeared as a wave pushing down on the river, and a fall of the flow in response to the push: visually depicted as a waterfall. The "river" label was further broken down into "flows, cold, clear, necessary for life, circulation, and etheric flow."

Two other images in figure 11.1 were also depicting this flow. The first was the "treelike object" in the bottom left. Associated terms perceived that related to the triangle and the treelike object were "circulates," "branches dark-to-light," "light-to-dark," and then outward movement at the base of both the tree and the triangle, along with the force shown by the arrows, which had more of a visceral feel of pushing down, and later movement at the base.

Cayce appears to be explaining how the forces are before the stone is used as a facilitator for change. The diagram of these forces in figure 11.1 shows a natural force that is resisted by an unspecified force that moves in a lateral direction instead of in opposition.

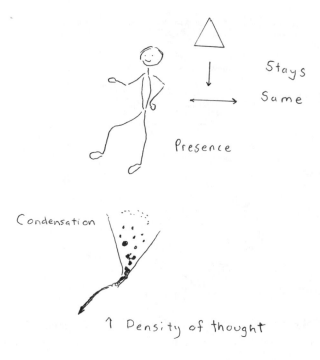

**Figure 11.2**

The focus in the second sketch is on two images (figure 11.2). The first is a triangle next to a *presence*. The triangle is the same as the one that appeared above the river of etheric flow in the previous drawing. The spirit contact presents the triangle as the ideogram of the element of air. Because "air" and "element" are labels, I break the terms down into descriptive terms: "action, thought, intention, movement of the mind flow into water." This label breakdown is not completely consistent with the traditional meaning of air, but it is what I perceived to be the interpretation of this symbol.

Cayce then presents an image of water condensing from the air and flowing with ever greater density and opacity until it is flowing as a solid mass. The image of this condensation and flow is below the perception of presence in figure 11.2. Cayce highlights a *presence*. This presence is a nonspecific humanlike presence. It could be anyone. The symbolic triangle presented in the first sketch plus the presence in figure 11.2 are combined to show a state of equilibrium of the presence. So the first sketch and the top of the second sketch symbolize a presence that is in a state which is stable and unchanging. I believe the esoteric symbolism indicates that this is an etheric or spiritual energy state.

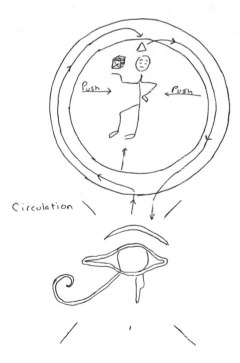

**Figure 11.3**

The third sketch shows the patterns of how thought flows in and out of the Nexus (figure 11.3). The etheric river is a boundary between the human, physical world and the Nexus, represented by the outer area. The human in the center is restricted by this etheric boundary. The inner area represents the limited area of physical manifestation. The image of the natural force in figure 11.1 is depicted in action in figure 11.3.

*Circulation* is defined by Cayce as flowing etheric energy. This term was used by him frequently in readings, but it was never defined as clearly as he has done here. The focus is now on the *presence*. It relates how thought moves by intention through the creative process and interaction with the Nexus.

*Post-session interpretation:* This session relates to crystals, in that the crystal has to go through this same process in order to essentially program it for its purpose. By the end of the channeling session, Cayce corrects the idea of "stone" that was in the original inquiry to the idea of a crystal.

The Eye of Horus was a specific image that prevailed as the source of the "juice," so to speak, that powers the universe—the presence, and the object held by the presence. I did not feel that this symbol was used exactly according to its traditional meaning, so I broke it down into "all-seeing, creative power, defense, source of life." It is a combination of the all-seeing eye symbol and the traditional Egyptian symbol. It is also characteristic of Edgar Cayce—Atlantean and ancient Egyptian lore came up quite frequently in his readings while he was living on the earth.

**Figure 11.4**

After perceiving the imagery Cayce presented, seen in figure 11.3, I asked for more clarification: "Describe how you make changes using this model." The clarification is presented in figure 11.4. I perceived an image of a juggler. The label of "juggler" was then broken down into "not impeding flow, not focused on one object, keeps within, circulation by touch-and-release action, mind steady and focused, stillness and action, mind neutral in a place where it can observe, manipulate with calmness." I interpreted this as being a mental and emotional state—quiet, deep, persistent focus, flowing thought without impediment or excitement. Cayce gave me a sense of a wheel of colors, with an alchemy sort of feel to it, within the radius of the juggled objects.

At the time of the session, I did not know what the box-shaped objects were. Post-session, I felt they were crystals. The process is not literal juggling, but juggling is symbolic of the state of mind and process related to the initial inquiry.

The images cleared, and Cayce then presented a two-dimensional puzzle containing the idea that these pieces fit together as a whole. This is drawn below the image of the juggler in figure 11.4. The puzzle broke apart and appeared to be flowing in a stream, like liquid. The clairsentient feel is that this imagery is symbolic, and a continued expansion of the ideas presented in figures 11.3 and 11.4.

Even though these images are simple, there is a great deal of depth and meaning to them. In the post-session analysis, Cayce was projecting the very process of programming and using a crystal. This was done in such a way that more of the inner workings as to how the tuning process actually takes place was presented with greater clarity than I have ever seen before.

**Figure 11.5**

The puzzle in the flow continues to the next sketch, shown in figure 11.5. The presence is attempting to put the puzzle pieces together. The mind is calm, not focused on any one piece but on the movement that puts the pieces together. This then moves to a close-up of the puzzle, which now has a hole in it. The presence is trying to figure out what to do with the hole. This presence looks around for something that fits into the hole and finds the object, which is now placed into the hole and completes the puzzle.

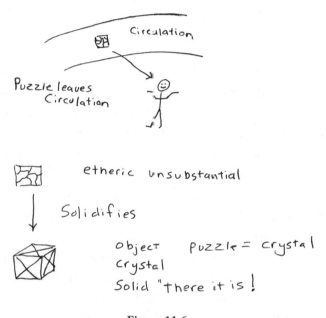

**Figure 11.6**

The puzzle now goes through the alchemical process of solidification, shown in figure 11.6. Remember, this little story is a parable that answers the initial inquiry of how a stone (now known as a crystal) creates change. This whole story has the clairsentient feel of an alchemical process. The individual crystals are not identified but appear to go through a process, and the process they go through has more to do with the changes they can facilitate than with the actual crystal itself.

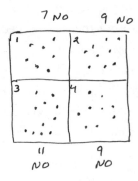

**Figure 11.7**

In this last sketch (figure 11.7), which was done after the session, I realized that the *object* was of some significance, so I dowsed to see if the identity of the object was more significant than the activity and energy of the *presence*. The trigger statement was "Describe through dot matrix dowsing whether the primary perception of *object* is more or less important than the primary perception of *presence*." Odd numbers are "no" and indicate less; even numbers are "yes" and indicate more. In all four squares, there was an odd number of dots, indicating that the identity of the *object* was less important than the energy and activity of the *presence*.

This case study gives a pretty good example of how conceptual inquiries are handled through sketching. The bulk of the information is in the images. Clairsentient feel is also important in relaying information. The images, if seen as a parable, can relay nearly all the information needed to answer the question. I wrote the interpretation of the sketches to help you see how images portray all kinds of information, including ideas and concepts. The material Cayce presented is intended to be a parable—a tool that was very familiar to him in life. I found him to be an excellent communicator, easy to connect with and clear in his presentation.

# CHAPTER TWELVE
# A CASE STUDY IN SESSION ANALYSIS: RAVEN SPIRIT

The case study presented in this chapter is shamanic in nature. I channeled a nonspecific raven spirit. In this session you see a local place through the eyes of this raven spirit. The raven spirit gives a very visual presentation. The idea of channeling an animal spirit was intriguing. Before I did the experiments related to this book, I had never channeled an animal spirit. It was a good test of the theory of the availability and unlimited access of information in an interactive mode that is characteristic of the Nexus.

Ravens are large black birds that live in areas with dense woods and hilly to mountainous terrain. On our property we have nesting ravens that have been here for at least ten years and probably more. The matriarch is nearly as big as a young bald eagle. They are intelligent animals and can be heard mimicking sounds from the nearby houses and farms in the area and watching human and animal activity with seemingly unending interest from the nearby trees. They mimic not only sounds but also human speech.

The raven spirit is a popular familiar in shamanic culture. In the Norse sagas, the ravens Huginn (Old Norse for *thoughts*) and Muninn (Old Norse for *memory*) are said to have roamed the world and reported back to Odin with the news they found. Odin gave them the ability to speak so they could whisper their news in his ears while they perched on his shoulders. The natural intelligence of this bird coupled with its role in folklore and myth make it a natural choice for a channeling session.

Keep in mind that the feedback interpretations included here were done after the channeling session was completed and the inquiry revealed.

I set up the session with five inquiries:

1. What does Round Lake, and features you find to be important there, look like at the time when I go to take a picture of the location (about 9:00 a.m. on the 10th of June, 2021)?

2. What does the grocery store from the parking lot in front look like when I am present to take a photo of the location (about 9:00 a.m. on the 10th of June, 2021).

3. What does the ocean beach north of the power plant look like, and what is important to you there, when I am present to take a photo of the location (about 9:00 a.m. on the 10th of June, 2021)?

4. How can I improve my channeling with you?

5. What do you like to eat best and how do you find it?

As you can see, these inquiries are very different from each other. I wrote these on equal strips of paper and put them in a bag. I drew one out at random and started the session. After the channeling session was done, I revealed to myself the inquiry that I had channeled and went to the location to take photos.

The question that was selected was the first one: "What does Round Lake, and features you find to be important there, look like at the time when I go to take a picture of the location (about 9:00 a.m. on the 10th of June, 2021)?" Round Lake is the local name for the lake and not what is on the map. It is a perfectly round lake and a popular swimming hole for locals. The lake has a running/walking trail that goes around it, a boat launching area, and a couple of picnic shelters.

## Channeling Session

I started the session with the short contact ritual from chapter 4. I did not do trance channeling. I started the session by asking for the primary perceptions. I intuitively felt an *object*, a second *object*, *activity*, and *concept*.

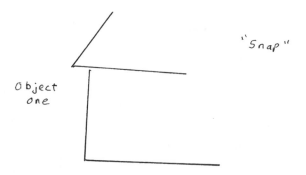

**Figure 12.1**

The object in figure 12.1 has characteristics of a structure. It is associated with a snapping sound. Ravens make a clapping sound with their beaks as part of their complex verbal communication with each other. The spirit contact was comparing this sound to beak clapping. I later interpreted the snapping sound as a car door closing.

**Feedback Photo 1**

In the feedback session, I interpreted this object to be a picnic shelter on the walkway to the beach (feedback photo 1). The parking lot is next to that shelter, and the sound of car doors closing was present at the time requested.

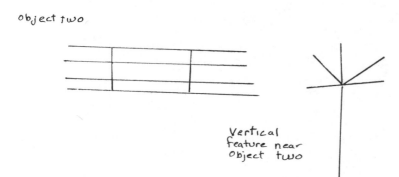

**Figure 12.2**

The second sketch shows a grid-like structure (figure 12.2). I interpreted it in the feedback session to be the footbridge over a small creek that goes from the path to the beach itself.

Objects 1 and 2 were then shown to me in context. As I perceived the objects, I realized that the colors were odd. I had difficulty describing them. I felt like I was seeing the place through the eyes of the raven, and it looked very different from what a human eye sees. The colors were bright and did not appear natural in that they had a fluorescent or metallic glow. Through this strange vision, I then was shown a vertical feature that was next to object 2.

The indication of the location of the objects was very precise. Knowing how the beach and parking area are laid out, I had no difficulty interpreting the objects in the session, even though the color effect was bizarre.

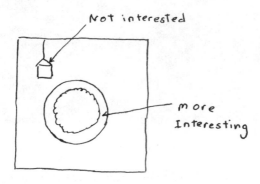

**Figure 12.3**

The third sketch shows context between objects 1 and 2 and the area immediately surrounding them (figure 12.3). The raven spirit indicated to me that it was not interested in the area containing objects 1 and 2, but rather in the area next to it. The raven spirit also expressed great interest in the ringed area around another object, which is defined later in the session. The *activity* relates to undefined presences in the air and on the ground. I asked the raven spirit, "Why is this area more interesting to you than objects 1 and 2?"

The spirit indicated that the second primary perception of *activity* was the response to the question. The activity appeared to be on the ground and in the air. The raven spirit felt happiness at the activity, and it felt as though the bird was eating and feeling satisfied.

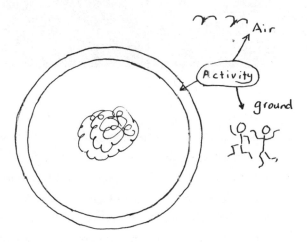

**Figure 12.4**

The fourth sketch shows additional context, with the primary perception of *activity* (figure 12.4).

**Feedback Photo 2**

In the feedback session, it was very clear to me that this activity relates to the footpath that goes around the lake (feedback photo 2). The picnic areas lie on the trail that goes around the lake and on the beach itself.

The raven spirit is indicating that it is attracted to the activity on the footpath. The lake is a recreation area, and it is not unusual for people to have picnics there. Ravens are scavengers by nature, so this does make sense to me. The green color of the landscape seems unnatural and even fluorescent. It looks like paintings people have made from visions in ayahuasca and peyote ceremonies. The raven spirit seems to be very focused on showing me how to find food at Round Lake.

12

11

12

10

**Figure 12.5**

I did a dot matrix dowsing (figure 12.5). The dowsing trigger was "Is the activity more important to you than objects 1 and 2?" The even numbers are positive responses and the odd numbers are negative responses. The first square contained twelve dots, which is a positive response, and the second square contained eleven dots, which is a negative response. The third square contained twelve dots, which is a positive response, and the fourth square contained ten dots, which is a positive response. The overall count is three squares with a positive response and one square with a negative response, so the answer is a positive response: the activity is more important to the raven spirit than the objects.

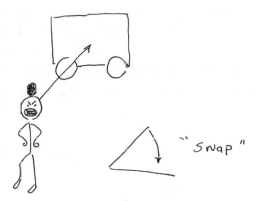

**Figure 12.6**

After I made this assessment, I then directed the spirit with the following: "Even though the activity is more important, I need you to look at one of the objects in this area and tell me as much as you can about it so that others can understand how to communicate with you."

The raven spirit shifted its focus to another object and decided to communicate information about it. Its reaction to the request was very positive. The spirit contact had enthusiasm for the communication and came across as a very joyful being throughout the session. It tended to shift focus very quickly from one thing to another. I had to slow things down a bit so I could get the sketches down on paper.

The primary perception of *concept* is closely related to object 3. In figure 12.6, the concept is a feeling of being trapped. That concept leads to a shape that appears very car-like and is a dark color. The car-like shape was broken down into "dark, bad, boxy shape, a loud booming sound, and a feeling of dread and entrapment." The trap is full of monsters, which are described as big birds that move funny. The hair on top of the monster's head is seen as a raised crest, which can be threatening, or the body language of a firm, explicative statement.

Any boxy shape, including the one in figure 12.1, is considered to be scary and something to be feared as a trap.

I then moved to a second concept. I asked the raven spirit to tell me more about the ideas related to the boxy car-shaped object. The concept is to avoid the trap and satisfy needs. So the spirit starts with the car-like object that contains scary monsters and is a trap to be avoided. The spirit associates the trap-like object with food but also with danger. There is a sense of worry, fear of monsters, fear of being trapped, and fear of hunger. This is shown by the ideogram of multiple question marks in the next sketch (figure 12.7).

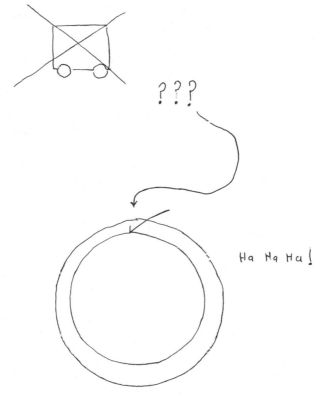

**Figure 12.7**

So what is to be done? This last sketch shows the raven spirit's solution to the problem. The contact shows me the double circle and projects an emotional atmosphere of "ha-ha, feel happy, no traps, I'm clever."

In the feedback session on figure 12.7, I interpret the path around the lake as a footpath. No cars are allowed on the path.

The last object is then presented to me by the raven spirit. It is a large, wet, grey, multilayered object. I sense that the spirit does not find this large, wet object interesting. It feels like it does not want anything to do with it, and moves past it when it encounters it. In the feedback session, this object appeared to be Round Lake itself. I did not bother to make a sketch of it due to its lack of specific features.

This concludes this session on the raven spirit. I gave the spirit a sense of appreciation and got up to find something to drink.

## CHAPTER THIRTEEN
# SPONTANEOUS CHANNELING

At this point you have the basics of a structured formal channeling session that will provide you with a good connection to your spirit contact, as well as precise information. These techniques apply to entities living in the Nexus, or spirit world, as well as to those who live physical lives but have a spiritual presence in the Nexus, as humans do. Animal spirits and extraterrestrials who live in the physical universe are two examples of physically based spirit contacts.

You have learned to use a grab bag and the importance of sketching and descriptive language in automatic writing responses. I have presented a couple basic dowsing techniques and the spirit board. You understand the session structure and the value of consistency and practice. You use the tools of feedback and calibration targets for reality checking. Both of these feedback tools provide a way to improve your channeling skills and point out where you are falling into belief and expectation biases and fantasy traps. I hope you have tried these skills and have felt empowered by them. By now you should realize that channeling is something you can do and that a door to a whole new universe has been opened for you.

As a result of the channeling you have done, you are now on the radar of spirit contacts who have made discoveries and are eager to share these with you. Once they become aware of you, these contacts will attempt to communicate with you when you are not in a formal session. There may be times when you perceive information that you want to check into more deeply. So what do you do? The formal channeling session structure does not seem relevant in this situation, because you have already been contacted by an entity and possess the information the entity wished to convey to you. In this chapter I will provide you with a means to validate information that is spontaneously perceived outside of a formal channeling session.

## The Nature of Spontaneous Channeling

When does spontaneous channeling happen? Most often it occurs at night during the hypnagogic state you are in when you first wake up from sleep. Spontaneous contact can happen several times over the course of a night. You are naturally receptive to spirits in this state, and those who are interested in communicating with you will take advantage of that openness to try to transmit information or interact with you. Any kind of daydream state is also fair game for spirits to try to communicate or interact with you. Spirit contacts generally prefer to use these natural trancelike states of consciousness because it is easier for them to get through to you when you are in these states.

For me, spontaneous channeling of a spirit is usually something that occurs after I have my first sleep cycle of the night. It happens to me most nights, and occasionally even during the daytime. Once you start channeling, you open a door that will not easily close. Personally, I would not want it to.

A spontaneous communication from the Nexus is usually experienced as a sense of suddenly knowing something. The first few times this occurs, the sensation will be more intense. After you have the experience a couple of times, you will get used to what it feels like, and the emotional intensity will not seem as great but the transmission will still come through. The intensity of the spontaneous experience does not appear to be related to accuracy of the channeled information. I have had very intense experiences that proved to be inaccurate when the information was reality-tested. There have also been times when the more intense experiences channeled accurate, precise information with a high degree of specificity and usefulness. So what I do is enjoy the intense experiences but balance them out with the more mundane, less exciting, but more accurate formal, structured channeling.

# Downloads

A *download* is a fairly common channeling experience that occurs during sleep. When you wake up, you find that you have acquired information without learning it in the normal way—that is, by reading, conversing, or doing an activity. Most everyone receives these downloads at some point in their lives.

Even before I developed clairaudience about ten years ago, I had experiences with these spontaneous downloads. After I acquired scrying and clairaudient skills, I also began to perceive the channeled information in sound and images. The big download type of channeling does not come across as sound and image, however. The download is a large quantity of complex information that is being channeled very rapidly. By contrast, the voices and images I perceive usually involve something very specific, with a narrow focus, or are interactions of a personal type rather than just exchanges of information.

Development of these "clair" abilities is possible even if you were not born with the talent. When you work in a consistent way with channeling of any sort, clair abilities will make themselves evident through deliberate action or they will happen spontaneously. However, the downloads, which contain large amounts of valuable information, are not perceived with normal clairaudience or clairvoyance. Even if you never develop the "clairs," your inherent ability to perceive information at a deep level is sufficient for this kind of spontaneous acquisition of knowledge.

## What Causes Spontaneous Channeling?

Once you are established on the Nexus radar as someone who has channeling skills, and the entities around you realize that you are interested in spirit communication, there is a tendency for those keen on interacting with living human beings to focus their attention on you. I think that human spirits in particular make discoveries when they die that they want people who are still alive to know about. Some may miss their friends and relatives as well. Direct communication with close friends and family who are still in the body is difficult when those persons have no psychic abilities, so human spirits may try to reach them through a recognized channeler.

Another reason for spontaneous channeling is that a spirit contact may wish to impart some specific bit of information to you that it was not able to convey to you during a formal session. It will wait for a time when you are mentally open to the download and then download the information into your head. Spirits cannot do this if you are not open to it. I can sense when this is happening, and if I do not want the information or do not want to interact with that spirit, then I just refocus and the spirit cannot interact in that way with me. Interaction is always voluntary or at least controllable by the channeler. It takes effort, focus, and stillness to keep the channel open, but it is relatively easy to break the connection.

I find that spontaneous channeling happens to me on most nights. Some nights it is only a greeting and brief interaction, but on other nights it can be more intense. There are times that it does not happen for a couple of months and times when it happens twice a day. In the latter case, fatigue can become a factor. These spontaneous interactions can disrupt sleep. After a night or two of them, I tend to crash and sleep too deeply for the interaction to occur.

There are times when I have good energy levels and a balanced life. During those times I will have these spontaneous events frequently. You cannot force the interactions. They happen when they happen. It is important that they not take the place of formal channeling sessions that are subject to feedback on real-time events and locations. Any significant real-time information obtained during a spontaneous channeling session that can be validated should be subjected to a formal reality-check channeling session.

## Is Spontaneous Channeling Harmful?

I find these spontaneous interactions with spirits to be helpful. I benefit from the deep personal companionship that is a result of the communication. There is potential for harm if the interaction is scary, or if it lures the channeler into a persistent fantasy or delusion. It could lead to a false diagnosis of a mental illness and subsequent treatment if the validation sessions are neglected. The key to avoiding problems is to always practice strict reality checks with the channeled information. Spirits who want to lead you into a delusion or fantasy will avoid interaction with people who do this.

Some spirits just want attention and seek to encourage belief-based systems with them at the center. The important thing is to decide what you want to believe, as a matter of faith, and change it only if you feel you need to change it. The spirits cannot force you into one belief or another. Sometimes they may try to scare you into a particular belief. Understand that this is not related to fact, but is just a form of mental manipulation to advance whatever agenda that spirit has.

This manipulation may not arise from any evil intent. I think that spirits, just like human beings, tend to believe that things are a certain way as a matter of faith, and act accordingly. For example, they may try to make you think you were chosen as a leader or are special in some way, and they will use a hundred little manipulative tricks to draw you into their world. If you want to be there, that's fine, but if you do not, then they cannot force you to be there. You choose what you want to do.

## The Importance of Formal Structure

In the method of channeling I teach in this book, the formal channeling session is at the heart of the work. Information that is subject to real-time feedback improves over time. Spontaneous experiences may add to the richness of your life, but they do not improve your accuracy as a channeler or the quality of the information you receive. Both spontaneous and structured sessions play important roles in your interaction with nonphysical entities and telepaths. If you only work with spontaneous channeling, you will be seeking more intense experiences without focusing on accurate, high-quality, practical information. You will tend to drift into fantasies, and possibly even into persistent delusions.

Issues with accuracy and bias have been problematic in the past when practicing mediumship. If you are looking to work with a group, you will need to develop a reputation as someone who is mentally and emotionally sound and who produces work of consistent quality. Even if you are working solo, you need to keep a foot on the ground of reality so that you can function, physically and socially, in the everyday world. It is important not to allow yourself to become lost in the sheer wonder of the channeling experience.

Meditation is a great tool. It intensifies your focus and improves your emotional and physical health. It helps you gain insights and is one of the building blocks of trance channeling. However, it will not make you more accurate. Meditation does not reduce the issues with belief bias and expectation bias. Trance has the same benefits as meditation, but it also does not necessarily make channeling more accurate. The trance state is better than normal waking consciousness for channeling manifestation energies, and also provides an experience with heightened richness and interest, but it does not produce data of better quality.

The first key to improve the accuracy, quality, and utility of the content of channeled material is blinding the conscious mind to the subject of inquiry. The second key is scrupulous physical, real-time feedback sessions for validation and verification of the received information. There are no exercises, no practices, no special diets, no incenses, rocks, enemas, or herbs that can facilitate the increased accuracy, quality, and usefulness of channeling as much as exclusion and proper feedback. You get better by practicing channeling in a way that shuts out the interpretive functions of your mind, and by continuing to do so consistently. I am advocating this system not just for beginners as a learning method. It is the channeling method I use personally, on a daily basis, and the method I teach regardless of the experience level or innate psychic talent of my students.

## Compassion

The first and foremost thing to remember when a spirit contacts you outside of a formal session is that it is a two-way relationship. The entity is a living being who has a mind and will of its own. It lives, thinks, and feels emotions. In some cases, the entity has influenced you at a deeper mind level because it is interested in a relationship, and this influence has caused you to move forward to put the channeling sessions together and allow the contact to begin. Being manipulated by spirits who have an agenda is less common than encountering spirits who are interested in friendship. Once you have the limits established and a good feedback system for spontaneous channeling, the spirits with an agenda will fade out of the picture.

Compassion is the first priority when it comes to spontaneous channeling. The entity is sharing part of itself with you. This is a personal and sometimes intimate experience emotionally. It is often an attempt to express affection and even love on the part of the entity. These experiences are almost always positive. Entities who do not like you or are not interested in a relationship generally avoid what they do not like or are not interested in. Most, if not all, of the time, the intention of a spirit who initiates spontaneous contact is positive and constructive.

Understanding and believing that most spirits have positive intentions is the first step in preventing misunderstandings between you and the spirit contact. Approaching a spontaneous channeling with compassion, and a realization that this is an entity that is opening itself and making itself vulnerable to you, will help you avoid unpleasant experiences. Focusing the mind in a positive way is essential. Fear, anger, and resentment are emotions that can create serious problems for someone who is just learning to channel and is starting to have personal experiences outside the framework of a formal session.

Negative emotions will color, and may even overwhelm, what you see in the entity, and you may perceive a well-intentioned contact attempt as a psychic attack. I have not seen any psychic attacks that did not stem from personal fears, anger, or hatred on the part of the channeler. Prevalence of these emotions in the makeup of any channeler will attract more of the same emotions. Even if the emotions raised are not in themselves entities, they will appear to be alive to the channeler. I had a great deal of trouble with this when I first became clairaudient a decade ago. As I learned to focus on positive emotions and eliminate negative influences in my life, things improved.

## Opening and Closing the Contact Door

Opening and closing your communication channel with a spirit is a particularly challenging aspect of channeling. Spirit contacts will come and go, and there are so many of them that want to talk to you that you could literally work day and night and still not get through all of them. The fact is, you need to do other things, such as eating and sleeping. You have to learn how to close the channeling door. If it is open all the time, you will not be able to sleep or function in your everyday life. If you keep the door open, you will constantly have a sense of spirits trying to reach you, touch you, or talk to you. You may even see them or see energy patterns related to their telepathic interactions, even if these are not intended for you.

Generally, when I have an issue with closing the spirit contact door, I get up and do something physical. Even if it is late at night, I go into the bathroom or read from a book that is unrelated to spirits for a bit before trying to go back to sleep. A change of focus will give your mind a chance to reset. It will not cause a problem when you go back to deliberate channeling. I take breaks for a month or two sometimes when I need to focus away from working with spirits. I have not had any issues coming back to channeling after taking a break. You do not lose the ability to channel. It is inherent in a human being. You can get a bit rusty. In that case, it only takes a session or two to pick up where you left off. You will not miss or lose anything if you shut down for a while. This is healthy and desirable to do. If you find you are not sleeping, then you need to back off and close the door until your mind and body reset.

## Validity Testing

Spirit contacts who come to you outside of a formal circle or session have something personal they want to share with you. This means, do not post it on social media. The spirit is sharing part of itself—it is a personal and private thing. Keep a log of any information the spirit gives you. Personal messages and interactions do not need validity testing. These are interactions with the spirit that are part of your private life, and it is best to leave it that way.

If a spirit imparts important information that you think others might be interested in hearing, that information needs validity testing *before* you share it. Confirming validity in channeling means that you have found the channeled information to have agreement with data you discovered through reading and researching credible documents related to the channeled information, and have tested it against other channeling sessions and/or against the data from other channelers. Validity testing is done using the three keys of exclusion, session structure, and feedback.

Validity testing of material received through spontaneous channeling is basically the same procedure as doing feedback on topic-based channeling. You need to assess the information and try to find out, through research of various kinds, whether or not it is accurate. Sometimes just a little research will turn up information that allows you to determine if a spirit communication is valid. This is probably the easiest way to do validation.

The secondary methods for validity testing involve checking your channeling experience to make sure the spirit actually did say what you thought it said. Because you are working with both the deeper mind and the superficial mind when you have spontaneous interactions with a spirit, you have an increased risk of belief and expectation biases. If these biases occur, you may hear and see something that you believe the spirit is communicating, but in reality you will be interacting with your own shadow—a fantasy created in your mind that looks like a spirit communication. Validity testing is the only sure way of telling the difference between actual communications versus belief and expectation biases or shadow fantasies.

You can make the following grab bag of questions for the spirit and do a channeling session using exclusion:

1. What did you channel to me on this date (day/month/year)?
2. What does this event (local event you are familiar with) on (day/month/year) look, sound, and feel like?
3. What does this local park (busy park you are familiar with) look, sound, and feel like?
4. What does this local water feature (river, beach, or waterfall known to you) look, sound, and feel like?
5. What will the weather be like here on (day/month/year in the near future)?

There will be a total of five questions in the grab bag. The primary question is an open-ended question that lets the spirit correct any information or add anything you may have missed during the original channeling. It is important not to be able to guess which question you have taken out of the bag. The questions need to be very different from each other. Insert specific places and dates into these questions to make them apply to your own experience. For the weather prediction, it should be within a few days and no more than a week into the future. The analysis and feedback session cannot be completed until the time has passed for the prediction to be revealed.

The procedure for this kind of session is a little different from that of a formal channeling session. Channel the spirit contact's response to all five questions in the grab bag before you reveal to yourself what the questions are. You draw out a question, set it aside unopened, channel it, and record your impressions, then draw out another question, set it aside, channel it, and record impressions, and so on. This is called *sequential channeling*. Complete the channeling on all five questions, one after the other, before you reveal the contents of the grab bag. This can be completed over the span of a couple of days. When you channel, use automatic sketching and writing, with dowsing for clarification. You do not need to make the sessions long. It is probably best to do just the normal waking consciousness channeling session because of the time involved in doing five sequential sessions. Be very careful to keep the slips of paper that bear the questions in their correct sequence so you do not get things mixed up.

Once you have finished working through all five slips in the grab bag, and the time for the weather prediction has passed, reveal the questions to yourself. Do feedback sessions on all the questions, including the first one about the spontaneous channeling experience. The other four calibration questions will give good factual feedback and will keep you on track for the primary question. You will see the differences between the channeling experience you had spontaneously and the validation channeling session.

When you do this validation consistently, you will find that you improve the quality of your channeling outside of a formal session. When you first do this, it might trip you up a bit. There is a sort of reality shock that occurs if you are channeling belief bias or expectation bias. It is like a splash of cold water in the face. That reality shock will put you back on track and clean out the channel, so to speak.

## Consensus Validation

*Internal consensus validation* is when the data from a channeling session is compared to data received during your other channeling sessions. You ask yourself, "Is this data consistent with the other data I have been receiving from this spirit contact?" It is helpful to maintain detailed, precise records of all your channeling sessions so you can do this. I recommend that validity testing be used along with consensus validation so that you can detect and correct channeling errors.

After multiple sessions with a spirit contact, consistencies start to become apparent. It is usually presumed that if something is consistent, it is reality or it is accurately channeled information. This assumption is not correct all the time. Consensus data is usually pretty accurate, but it is still vulnerable to belief and expectation biases. It is not perfect, and it does not work as well for feedback as impartial, factual information about physical places and events. However, in situations where you do not have any real-time information, consensus validation is the only available choice.

Validation can also be achieved by comparing the channeled data with data received during sessions conducted by other channelers. This is called *external consensus validation*. An example of external consensus data is the association of a particular philosophical element with one of the compass directions in the Golden Dawn system of magic. In this esoteric system, east is associated with elemental air. There are also certain symbols, colors, and psychological characteristics linked with the air element, such as the Tarot suit of swords, along with the colors yellow and violet. Air also symbolizes the intellect and thought. This is *external consensus data*.

If you are using the Golden Dawn system to validate your work, you would compare the results of your channeling to information on the topic in the Golden Dawn set of occult correspondences. The Golden Dawn consensus information comes from research of manuscripts, the teachings of Theosophy, and other esoteric sources. Material was also channeled or scryed by members of the Golden Dawn. So in this case you are checking your work against individuals who had a reputation for accuracy in their channeling and scrying. Does that mean these people were correct? Maybe or maybe not. This illustrates the idea behind external consensus validation. Use it with caution.

To recap, if you have an experience with a spirit outside of a formal session, it is called spontaneous channeling. This can be a personal interaction or a download of information. Information received from this type of channeling session should be reality-tested through either normal feedback of the same kind, which is used in regular channeling sessions; internal consensus feedback, which compares the consistency of the channeled information across multiple sessions with a spirit; or external consensus, which compares the channeled information to what others have perceived. Spontaneous channeling is generally positive as long as the spirit contact does not disrupt the life of the channeler or attempt to manipulate the channeler into changing their beliefs.

# CHAPTER FOURTEEN

# FRONT-LOADING

When working with channeling, there will be times when the grab bag system becomes inconvenient. For example, you may want very specific information quickly and have insufficient time to set up the inquiries. So how can you move past the hidden target system? For those who have practiced with occultation and are proficient with the grab bag system, it is possible to train for partial conscious knowledge of the inquiry. This is called *front-loading*.

I am borrowing this term from remote viewing, but it is an excellent term that describes what this chapter is about. In remote viewing circles, front-loading is when you remote-view with knowledge of the target or inquiry prior to the session. In channeling I will describe front-loading the same way. It is channeling without using exclusion, or only partially excluding your conscious mind from the inquiry information.

Few remote viewers will attempt to train for front-loading because it is frustrating, difficult to do, and detrimental to your ability to work accurately if you do too much of it. In other divination disciplines, including channeling and mediumship, front-loading is commonly done.

I believe that front-loading as a normal channeling practice is why communications with spirit contacts are not consistently accurate. The interpretive mental processing completely overwhelms the communications from the spirit through the Nexus. Often you see a hodgepodge of a few accurate tidbits mixed with fantasy, bias, or worse. The result for the channeler is confusion, frustration, and discouragement, along with irritation on the part of the spirit contact, who cannot make its true responses known to the channeler.

Front-loading is an advanced skill. You need to be proficient with the channeling techniques using exclusion before ever attempting to work with it, if you decide to work with it at all. Before attempting front-loading, here are three cautions you need to keep in mind:

1. You will *never* eliminate the risk of belief and expectation biases. Even with exclusion, there is still a risk that they will taint the channeling session. Your biases are deeply ingrained, and your mind always processes and interprets all incoming information regardless of its source. The risk of contaminating the data is lessened when the mental processing mechanism is excluded from having information but is not eliminated. If exclusion is reduced or is not used, then the likelihood of channeling your beliefs and expectations increases.

2. Your accuracy in channeling will be inversely proportional to the amount of knowledge you have about the inquiry. As your front-loading knowledge increases, your accuracy in channeling decreases.

3. Your ability to channel accurately diminishes the more frequently you use front-loading. Normal mental interpretation will always be dominant over channeled input, and will always attempt to process and interpret the spirit contact's communication in line with beliefs and expectations. The inevitable result is distortion of the channeler's perceptions. The more often you front-load, the less accurate your channeling sessions become. You are hardwired this way. It is related to how the human brain processes information.

In light of these factors, you will appreciate that front-loading is a challenging skill in channeling. Is it even worthwhile to train for situations where you have some knowledge of the inquiry? Actually, yes, it may be worth it, because there are times and circumstances when the inquiry cannot be hidden and the information sought from the spirit contact is of vital importance. All the problems with front-loading being clearly understood, here is how you train.

You need to be familiar with the normal channeling procedure and be able to channel with confidence using the basic techniques presented in this book.

You also need to be able to channel accurate information on calibration inquiries. If you are not consistent with inquiries that can be verified during feedback, that is the first hurdle you must overcome before adding front-loading to your range of skills. Topic-based channeling needs to be a mastered skill. If you have that under your belt, then you can train for front-loading.

## Reality Shock Exercise

Reality shock is the only exercise I have in this book. It is done to prepare yourself for working with front-loading. Because front-loading is a challenging skill, it is necessary to do a bit of training work in order to master it. You work with the grab bag and a list of four inquiries. All four inquiries need to be completely verifiable. You put in three similar inquiries and one verifiable but very different inquiry. For example, if you are asking about a political situation, put in three questions regarding the political situation and one question about a beach in Florida. The contrasting inquiry has to be extremely different from the other three similar questions. The contrasting inquiry should be different in appearance and character. The feedback session that takes place after channeling is the key to this exercise.

Do sequential channeling on all four of the targets in the grab bag, working with the same spirit contact for all of them. You do not have to do this in one big session. You can work over a few days, or with multiple sessions in a day. Work the channeling sessions in detail, including trance channeling if you have time.

Draw a folded slip containing one of the questions, then work the channeling session. Without revealing what is on the slip of paper, set the channeling session aside with it and draw another slip out of the bag. Do the channeling session for the second slip. Continue to work through all the slips in the grab bag without revealing what is contained on the slips. You will at some point draw the contrasting reality check question from the grab bag.

After you finish channeling all four questions, reveal to yourself what is on the slips of paper. Make sure to keep the slips in order so you know which belongs with which session and do not get them mixed up. Find the session for the contrasting inquiry. Do light feedback on the three questions that were similar. The feedback session on the contrasting inquiry needs to be done in detail, perception by perception, and with complete honesty.

At first you will find that the channeling session for the reality check question is not as accurate as the other sessions. You may even bomb that session. If the session is completely off base, that's fine. It will still accomplish the goal of the reality check.

As you work through the feedback session, you will be exposing your biases. Feedback is what exposes your weaknesses but at the same time develops your strengths as a channeler. Doing feedback on concrete inquiries allows you to determine with certainty whether your channeled information was right or wrong, and, if it was inaccurate, by how much. You will be able to access very deep into your mind when you do this. The effect of the reality check is that it will clear out mental and emotional obstacles between you and your spirit contact.

When you look over your channeling session perception by perception during feedback, comparing it with the factual data, you will find that the majority of your bombed session is inaccurate, but there will be little pieces and tidbits that are spot-on. You need to mentally go back through your session and remember what it felt like when you wrote down those little bits that were accurate. After you do this a couple of times, you will begin to have sessions with more of those accurate bits. This is the type of practice session that needs to be done periodically when you are doing front-loaded channeling.

Let's assume that you have had a few reality shock sessions and are not getting tripped up so easily. You find that you can pull the trick question and channel the information on it fairly accurately. Now what do you do?

## Basic Front-Loading

Start with inquiries about which you do not have a great deal of background information but on which you could easily discover that information. For example, ask the spirit to describe to you the car that is parked closest to your grocery store at the time in the future when you next go grocery shopping. When you go shopping the next time, take note of the car parked closest to the store and compare it to the spirit's description. In this way you will have exact knowledge of what you are looking for, but there is an unknown component to the inquiry that you have to discover. The channeling session is focused on that unknown bit of information.

Little jumps into the future are the best way to do this training. Predicting mundane things like the appearance of a car in a certain location, the outcome of a sports competition, or future weather are good ways to start working with front-loading. As you get used to doing this, you can expand your inquiries to include other things. The key is to try to focus on that one unknown aspect that you are seeking to find information about while ignoring the known aspects of the inquiry.

Known aspects of the query are not what you desire to channel information on. You can find out such information using your research skills, so why would you resort to channeling? It is the mysterious aspects in the midst of the known information that you seek to investigate. You have to learn to ignore the known bits of information and focus on what you do not know.

The next part of the front-loading training strategy is to use the same structure that you would use in a topic-based channeling session. Instead of focusing on the inquiry, you identify the primary perceptions just as you would when you do an unknown inquiry. The session structure and focus are exactly the same. The exposed tasking, which is hidden normally, will now be written something like this: "What is the nature and appearance of the (person/place/event/concept)?"

You will continue to channel in descriptive language, breaking down labels in just the same way you do for a regular hidden-topic channeling session. The focus of the session should be on sketching, with descriptions used to elaborate on the sketches.

The spirit contact will usually go through very fine details, and the snapshot of the response will be almost too finely focused. It is necessary in most cases to step back and take a broader look at the inquiry. If you find that you are not getting complete information, then the contact is probably doing this microscopic examination. Ask it to step back and give you a broader picture.

When you make this transition to using front-loading, start with the grab bag technique and basic channeling. Proficiency with the basic technique is essential before using front-loading techniques. When you do a front-loaded session, work the inquiry with the contact in the same way you do in a normal channeling session that has a hidden objective. In between your front-loaded sessions, go back frequently to using a grab bag with at least four hidden inquiries until you are no longer tripped up when you channel information on the trick inquiry that is planted in the bag. If you find yourself constantly battling to get accurate results when you do this front-loading technique, stay with the grab bag method for a while. Do not fight with this difficulty to the point of burning yourself out.

Working with front-loading will teach you a great deal about your inner beliefs. It is a great tool to use for spiritual development and insight, and is one of the most enlightening things you can do for yourself. Once you have identified your inner tendencies, and know when they are coming into play during a channeling session, you can learn to avoid their influence to some degree.

The technique I have described here does not supplant the grab bag technique for accuracy. Going in with a hidden inquiry will always be the most accurate and easiest way to work with channeling. Some people will find that the battle with front-loading is just too frustrating to deal with. That's okay. Success with front-loading depends a great deal on your patience, time, and frustration tolerance. If it gets to the point where channeling is not enjoyable, go back to the grab bag technique. Feedback sessions will still reveal a great deal about your inner heart and help enlighten you with insights when doing hidden inquiries. You can always try again at a later date. It took me a couple years of constant work before I was able to tolerate front-loaded sessions. Even today, I feel just a bit of liver twitching when I go into a channeling or scrying session with front-loading.

## Partial Front-Loading

Another technique for learning front-loading is to do part of a session the usual way with a concealed target, then reveal what the inquiry is when you are about halfway through the session. In this way you start with proper focus and you will find that you are less likely to stray when the information is revealed.

To train for partial front-loading, start with the reality check grab bag. As before, have three questions in the bag that are related to the same topic and one question about a time/space/event that is completely different in character and appearance from the first three. Work each question with the spirit until you have drawn all four inquiries out of the grab bag. Then find your trick question and go over it in detail. If you have a good session with that inquiry, then you are ready to start your work with partial front-loading.

## Technique for Basic Partial Front-Loading

First, you will do the pencil and paper session, and you will work with a grab bag of four questions. Take a slip of paper out of the grab bag and start your session just like you do during a normal hidden inquiry session. When you get about halfway through your session, look at what you drew out of the grab bag.

Refocus and continue your paper session. Mentally place your focus exactly where you left off, as if you did not know what the inquiry was. The idea is to keep your focus on the primary perceptions at all times during the session.

Ask your contact to show you the aspects of the topic that you do not have knowledge about. Use this trigger: "Describe any information that I need to write down." Continue to focus on sketching and descriptive language. Treat labels just as you would for a normal grab bag session, breaking them down into descriptive terms.

When you do feedback, make sure to note areas that turn out to be inaccurate. It is important for the first few partial-front-loading channeling sessions that you work with grounded inquiries that provide rich material for a good feedback session. The unknown aspects of the inquiry should be things you can look up or research. The goal here is to use the feedback to determine channeling weaknesses, expose biases, and reveal problems with focus. You are calibrating your channeling as you channel.

## Reducing Grab Bag Entries

The preparation for this front-loading technique is the same as for basic front-loading and partial front-loading. You want to channel information using the reality check grab bag to the point where you channel information on the trick question with the same accuracy as you do during a regular channeling session with the inquiry hidden.

Normally you would start with at least four entries in the grab bag. To reduce grab bag entries, you start with one entry less than what you normally use, and you do not reveal the subject of inquiry during the session. Instead, you complete your session and then reveal what the topic was supposed to be. If you do well with, say, three entries in the grab bag, then reduce the number to two for the next channeling session. Once you can do two, then do not hide the question.

The focus of the session should be on the primary perceptions, even when you know the inquiry. Keep the session structure exactly the same as for basic channeling. Use sketches and descriptive language. Break down labels into descriptive language. Hunt for unknown aspects of the topic, and focus on those areas. The feedback session should focus on the unknown aspects, and for the initial sessions the inquiries should be grounded and verifiable. Predictions should be very short-term for the first few sessions.

## Front-Loading Esoteric Inquiries

As I said before, the nature of esoteric inquiries is very subjective. These can be inquiries regarding certain occult properties such as the nature of the philosophical elements, astrology, Kabbalah, and so on. The feedback can be tricky when you do esoteric inquiries. It is more likely that you will find yourself moving into belief and expectation biases than when you're working with more concrete inquiries. You can work with esoteric inquiries using all the front-loading techniques discussed so far.

With esoteric inquiries, you often have to rely on consensus feedback to a greater extent than you normally would with a concrete inquiry. This type of feedback is considerably less effective, especially when you add front-loading to the mix. The best way to avoid problems with accuracy is to select inquiries very carefully, and try to have partially verifiable concrete information related to those inquiries. It is important to alternate between esoteric inquiries and concrete verifiable inquiries when you get to this point in your training or if you have a special interest in esoteric topics.

Having sessions on topics for which you cannot do an effective feedback session will, in time, cause deterioration of accuracy due to overpowering from mental processing and biases. Training for front-loading is one of the very few times when I recommend that you do exercises to hone your skills. Working with a reality check is the exercise I recommend most if you want to practice front-loaded channeling sessions. I find that if I do one trick question session for every two esoteric inquiries, I can maintain my channeling accuracy fairly well.

## Summary of the Reality Check Exercise for Front-Loading

Reality check for front-loading is an exercise used to help the medium reveal belief and expectation biases and aid in preventing them from overwhelming the spirit's subtle communication. Here is a summary of the key points of this exercise.

1. Be practiced in regular channeling before attempting front-loading.
2. Be proficient at the reality check exercise given in this chapter.
3. Start with partial front-loading.
4. Select a total of four verifiable questions for the reality check grab bag. Three questions will be on the same topic and one question will be a trick question—that is, a time/location/event type of inquiry having a completely different character and appearance from the other three questions.
5. Do channeling sessions on all four questions before revealing which one was pulled from the grab bag.
6. Find the session for the trick question and do a very detailed feedback on that question. Go through the session perception by perception, noting the accurate and inaccurate information.
7. When you can handle the trick question accurately, then you are ready to start working with front-loading.
8. Start front-loading training with small jumps into the future.
9. When front-loading, mix it up with grab bag sessions as well to keep your skills up.

# CHAPTER FIFTEEN

# GROUP PRACTICE

In this chapter I will go over considerations for channeling with a group. The material in this book can be used by a solitary practitioner or a small group of two to eight people. Groups that practice channeling, scrying, and magic usually meet in the members' homes. Not all homes can accommodate more than eight people comfortably. For this reason, if there are more than eight people who wish to channel together, I suggest dividing into two smaller groups.

The traditional approach for groups focused on channeling has been to use a single person as the focus of the group. This special medium did all the channeling. The rest of the group participated in a minimal way by lending the channeler their moral support and mental focus. The atmosphere was that of a group of people being entertained by a performer. The Spiritualist Church still works this way. While I think this tradition is valid, and an important part of the history and practice of channeling, I find that equal participation by all members of the group is a better way to go.

Since the mid-1990s I have participated in what is called Human-initiated Extraterrestrial (HiET) contact, also known as CE-5 experiments. These are channeling sessions where a group of people meet in what is usually an outdoor setting and attempt to contact extraterrestrial intelligences for the purpose of asking them to show themselves by flying their craft (UFOs) across the sky above the heads of the group.

The group works as a unit to attract the attention of extraterrestrials who have craft within range, and tries to persuade them to fly over the group so that their presence can be witnessed and recorded. The participation of every member of the group is important. During an outing, the group will do a guided meditation for several hours. My own experiments related to HiET have been successful and have resulted in some fascinating experiences. A number of organizations are involved in running these experiments, with the oldest of the still active organizations being Rahma, based in Peru.

It is this philosophy of equal participation and universal talent that I use as a guide for my group channeling work. Each member of the channeling circle has the ability to learn how to channel. They also have the right to participate in the channeling session. Everyone in the circle is a spirit that is living a physical life. Each spirit can commune with all other spirits. Active participation is required to be present in the sitting.

## Setting Up a Channeling Circle

Let's say you want to set up a channeling circle. How do you go about doing that? First, you need a place to work. The only places to avoid are locations where you will be interrupted and the place where you sleep, unless you live in a one-room apartment or a hotel room. In that case, you will have to work with your group where you sleep. You will need space for a table and some chairs. The chairs need to be set around the table so that participants face each other. The ideal number for a channeling group is four people. Adequate quantities of pencils, paper, and drawing implements such as color markers should be at the center of the table. A grab bag is essential. A dowsing pendulum is an option if the group wants to do pendulum work. For every table of four people, one spirit board can also be used.

## Ground Rules

There is nothing more annoying than someone who comes into a channeling group to try to disrupt or challenge the group. To help prevent this, all the participants should be known to the person setting up the group. Pick people who are willing to participate. There should be no bystanders. Enforcing participation will usually prevent problems with attitudes or personal agendas.

Requiring everyone to work together also discourages destructive antisocial behaviors such as debunking. Debunking is where someone asserts that they are an expert and tells the group members that they are not in contact with a spirit, regardless of the evidence presented. Having questions about channeling is normal, but debunking is a pathological extreme.

Distractions from the work need to be reduced or eliminated as much as possible. This is especially true regarding cell phones. The electronic pollution emitted from cell phones is destructive to channeling sessions.

All electronic and battery-operated devices that are not essential to the health and well-being of the group members (examples of essential devices would be a pacemaker or hearing aids) need to be placed at least ten feet from where the group is working. Ideally, they should not be in the same building, but that is not a reasonable expectation in most situations.

Ideally, channeling should be done where there is no EMF (electromagnetic field) at all, but this is nearly impossible unless you go camping deep in the wild. Even then, you are usually still within reach of a cell tower or some other source of electronic pollution. Once your group is well established, you should try to find a location to work that has no EMF pollution. You may be surprised at the difference this makes in the quality and accuracy of your channeling.

## Outdoor Channeling Sessions

Channeling sessions can be conducted indoors or outdoors. Most people prefer working indoors. However, in good weather the group may want to move outside. The basic procedure and equipment for working outdoors is the same as with an indoor group. Inquiries directed at the spirit contact are written out in the proper format and put into a grab bag. The focus of the session is on the primary perceptions of *object*, *presence*, *activity/energy*, and *concept*. Spirit-directed sketching is the highest priority. When something is written down, use descriptive language and break down any labels into descriptions. I will offer a few additional suggestions for groups that want to experiment with outdoor work.

You will need the grab bag, pens or pencils to write and draw with, paper for recording perceptions, and a table and chairs. You can use a picnic table if you have access to one. The spirit communication board is optional, as is dowsing. Channeling sessions that are based outdoors require a few additional pieces of equipment and involve some environmental considerations. When I conduct an outdoor session, I almost always have a campfire, with the group sitting in a circle around it. The selection of the subject of inquiry from the grab bag needs to be done before going outside. The slip of paper with the inquiry and the book being used should be nearby.

The facilitator will verbally guide the group through the individual steps of the channeling procedure, such as asking the trigger questions and writing the individual responses. It is important for the members of the group to trust in their personal responses and make sure to state them, even if they are not the same as what the other members have said. When you are group channeling on one inquiry, different perspectives will be given by different individuals. The entity or spirit can respond to multiple inquiries at once, since it is not limited by time and space in the Nexus.

Some believe that a spirit contact's responses have to be linear and occur one at a time, instead of happening to a group, with multiple mingled inquiries and responses. What appears to take place in group work is that the group receives a compressed download from the spirit contact, and they then individually break down, decompress, and describe the content of the download. There will be individual variation in the session content. After the group has been through this a few times and begins to understand how the information is being relayed, individual members should feel more comfortable describing things differently from others in the group.

The ideal spot for working outdoors is a dispersed camping site or a boondocking tent site. These campsites do not have utility hookups and are usually the farthest from the main store or activity center in the campground. You can use a large eight-person tent, setting up a camp table and chairs inside the tent. You will then have a bug-proof and rain-proof shelter. I would use LED flashlights for lighting needs, as fuel and flame lamps, live candles, and incense are not safe to use inside a nylon tent. For a group of four to six people, it takes about half an hour to set up the tent and be ready to work.

Another good site for this type of work is a picnic shelter, which provides considerable protection from the elements and can be resorted to if the weather becomes rainy. Picnic shelters often have a fireplace, which can provide a little warmth as well. I have also worked on beaches. The thing you have to watch out for when working on a beach is that it can get very wet, even if you are away from the water. Sand is unpleasant. It gets into everything. You also will have more wind on a beach, which is a problem when you are trying to write.

## Group Channeling Procedures

Group work adds to the individual channeling experience. All members of the group should be familiar with the process and able to do a solo channeling session before working together on a project. The first priority is to make sure that the group members have accomplished this step. Every member of the group is expected to contribute to the session. This means that everyone in the group needs to be trained in the channeling procedure.

For channeling practice groups, working with the grab bag technique and exclusion is just as important as it is for solitary practitioners. The procedure for a group channeling session is basically the same as for an individual's session. The individual members will all contribute to the session data by providing an inquiry for the spirit who will be channeled by the group during the session. The content of the inquiry will depend on the skill level of the group. For a beginner group, topics need to be ones that will provide the group with high-quality feedback. The channeled responses should be verified by research.

When you do the feedback session and find out what you did well and also what you did poorly, you will experience a reality check. This reality is helpful in understanding the channeling experience because it makes a distinction between perceptions that arose from bias and perceptions that were channeled from the spirit. Some perceptions will be accurate and some not. This can be an intimidating and bracing ordeal for the inexperienced channeler. The group members should be gentle with each other during the feedback session. Feedback is for learning, not stoking egos or bullying those who are having difficulty. Again, the fear of making mistakes in front of other people needs to be overcome, as does the desire for notoriety or fame.

All individuals in the group need to contribute to the grab bag. The group should discuss the types of spirits they want to work with and also what type of spirit they feel comfortable with. Generally, you should not channel a spirit if any member of the group is uncomfortable with that spirit. Group work can increase the intensity of the channeling experience, as well as increase the possibility of a supernatural manifestation. The spirit contacts that the group is working with need to be ones that are not threatening to the individual members.

In a group setting, it is usually best to work primarily with automatic writing and triggers formulated by the group. The best practice is to keep the session as simple as possible and work with the core skills of automatic writing and sketching. The focus of the group can determine what additions should be made as the group advances and wants to try different techniques. The addition of trance channeling, dowsing, and the spirit board is optional.

Automatic writing and sketching will give consistent and detailed information and are simple to use. If the group wants to try a different skill, go to trance channeling first. Dowsing can be done, but sometimes it can make the session too complex to be enjoyable. I feel that for group practice, the techniques should be kept simple, and the focus should be on the development of the most comprehensive and easy-to-learn skills.

## Compilation of Data

After the individual group members have finished with their sessions, the group facilitator will then compile all the information into one document. To compile the data, the group leader will write out the primary perceptions of *object*, *presence*, *activity/energy*, and *concept*. Each primary perception will have its own sheet of paper. Perceptions from the individual participants will fit into one or more of these four main categories. The facilitator should write them down under the appropriate category headings. Sketches are a priority. Sketches made by an individual should be copied by the facilitator of the group.

All perceptions should be included, even if there are duplications. There are always perceptions that seem out of place when compilation is done. This happens because the spirit will channel different perspectives, and the individual channelers will perceive from different perspectives. The contrasts are usually intentional by the spirit, and add to the overall picture of the information the spirit wants to convey.

The identity of the individual who gave the perceptive data should not be on the facilitator's compilation sheet. Group channeling is a collective experience in which all individuals contribute to the work as a whole. The process of compilation needs to be gentle. Individuals need to understand that they perceived what they perceived for a reason. Everyone will have aspects of their perceptions that can be validated and aspects that cannot be validated. Determining which is which must be done in a nonjudgmental way or it will be a negative experience.

## Interpretation and Feedback

The interpretation of the information starts at the same time as the feedback. At this time, the slip of paper that was drawn from the grab bag is unfolded and the question disclosed to the group. Known information about the question should be compiled and the session data compared to what is known. The facilitator then goes through the session data perception by perception, comparing each to the known information. The interpretation process involves putting these pieces together. Usually the spirit will fill in the holes in the group's information on the topic. The group can weave together the known data plus the information the spirit channeled. Information that appears to conflict with the known data should not automatically be assumed to be a miss. The spirit may be correcting the knowledge base or adding a different perspective to it. The contrasts should be noted. Usually, as the group continues to channel the spirit, the meaning of the contradictory information becomes clear.

The group should reflect on the information obtained during the session. Careful recording is helpful if the group is attempting to obtain new information or esoteric information that cannot be easily verified by the current knowledge base. If predictions are made, they need to be kept in a safe place until the dates of their fulfillment have passed and their accuracy can be reality-checked. Feedback can be done both at the end of the session and later as information comes in regarding the topic being channeled.

## Trance Channeling

If the group wants to practice trance channeling as part of its channeling session, then all members of the group need to participate. It is important that the experience of trance channeling not be judged. Instead, group members should share their personal experiences without comparing themselves to others, and these experiences should be accepted by the group as valid trance channeling experiences. That being said, group trance channeling can be facilitated if one member of the group guides the group. The member who does the guiding should be offered a chance to go into trance, so the role of facilitator needs to be rotated.

Part of the experience of trance channeling is the interaction that occurs at a very deep level when the group is going into trance in unison, focusing on exactly the same thing at the same time. When this happens, it is intense and rewarding. This magic only happens when the individuals of the group are completely absorbed in the task of trance channeling and ignoring any distractions.

## Online Group Meetings

There are circumstances where there is no other option than to run an online meeting. In these situations, it is important to be familiar with the material so that you have good focus during the session. With understanding and training, the group can succeed using an online meeting format. The members of the group need to be proficient with the procedures and the basic channeling skills. This makes it less likely that members will get discouraged due to the added challenges inherent in attempting to channel while meeting online. I encourage face-to-face work whenever possible. The EMF from computers and cell phones is not helpful to channeling and creates an additional obstacle for the group.

## Eat, Drink, and Be Merry

The group should partake of food and drink after the rituals are finished. Channeling burns energy, so it is not a bad idea to have a healthy snack and a drink after working. Socializing after the session helps to build bonds between group members. These ties are important for achieving detail and depth of perception during the channeling session. The group needs to spend time together to build trust and cohesion.

CHAPTER SIXTEEN
# USE OF SETTING

Before adding these immersive setting elements to channeling sessions, it is important that you have developed the skills of spirit communication and channeling, as described in previous chapters, to the point where you can run though a basic channeling session without referring to this book.

The four categories of primary perception, which are *object, presence, activity/energy*, and *concept*, need to be memorized. If you are cued with primary perceptions, you should be able to formulate trigger questions for the spirit on your own. You need to be able to make a grab bag and write appropriate questions for it. You need to be comfortable with both successes and misses in the feedback session. Correcting mistakes made in channeling is the most important skill. When you find yourself influenced by your biases or drifting into fantasy, you need to understand what caused this to happen and how to correct it.

Once you have attained these basic skills, you can advance your work by adding elements of setting. I encourage you to experiment creatively with immersive settings.

## What Is an Immersive Setting?

Up to this point, you have been sitting at a desk or table with pencil and paper to do channeling sessions. This chapter is about adding elements of creative, immersive settings to the experience. Setting is basically how your surroundings look in the location where you are doing the channeling session. It also involves adding elements of esoteric ritual to the experience of channeling.

For example, if you wanted to do a session in a traditional parlor room séance style, you would set a table in the center of the room, illuminate it with candles, and provide sketches or photos of the spirit contact. A spirit board is very appropriate for this style. You might even want to dress up for the part in vintage clothing of the late nineteenth century, when these séances became popular. Adding elements of setting is basically like dressing a stage for the activity of channeling. If you were acting in a play, you would want the stage to look like the setting described in the script. Use of setting in channeling creates mood in much the same way it does for a theater play.

Setting can have a significant psychological effect on the channeling experience. It creates an immersive experience. It takes the rather mundane exercise of sitting at a table and injects creative elements that affect you emotionally. Heightened emotion adds a degree of excitement and anticipation to the channeling session. It gives the experience color and style and strengthens the emotional connection to the spirit contact. It is a way to be creative and expressive in your channeling work.

I encourage original thinking and creativity in the use of channeling settings. I will present four basic setting styles that are based on well-known traditions. However, this is just a starting place. Use your unique creativity to develop your own individual style. Mix and match what you read here and what you find in your studies. The engagement of the creative process of your mind is what will make the setting work for you. I will go into the bare-bones basics of each tradition, its creative elements, and the spirits associated with it.

For example, you could choose the shamanic tradition and create a cave dwelling setting, and use that to channel dinosaurs or early hominids. It may sound a little silly, but you may be surprised at how that experience feels. If you like the ancient astronaut theory, you could create an early Mesopotamian setting and channel extraterrestrials using elements of that historical location, its artifacts, and literature pertaining to that period. You could then work through the human-initiated extraterrestrial contact ritual. This is simply the spirit contact ritual from chapter 4, but instead of a spirit, you are attempting to contact a physical, spiritual, or interdimensional extraterrestrial entity. I am giving you ideas for a stage that will support the drama of your channeling session. Create your own setting and have fun with it.

This creation of a stage setting for channeling is actually supported by parapsychology studies. The famous Philip experiment in Toronto in the 1970s was at first a failure until the team added elements of immersive setting to their sessions. They started to work with a nineteenth-century Spiritualist setting, complete with table tipping. While they had been in a circle meditating, nothing had happened. It wasn't until they added the immersive séance setting that the table used for the table tipping part of the session started to vibrate and move on its own. The Philip experiment team were following recommendations from various articles published in the *Journal of the Society for Psychical Research*.[10]

## Role of Spiritual Belief

You may have noticed that in the structure of the basic channeling sessions I do not present any particular point of view or belief about who or what spirits are. Both the psychological model of spirits and the independent spirit model have been presented in this book. You do not have to have any particular beliefs about spirits to succeed in channeling, whether you are doing a paper and pencil session at a desk or you have added immersive settings. As is true of my scrying method, presented in *The Art of Scrying and Dowsing*, there is no requirement to follow a particular spiritual path, or even to have any spirituality, to perform the experiments successfully. Adding an immersive setting is a way of using your creativity to engage you more emotionally and psychologically in the process of channeling. It will enhance the experience.

## Why Use an Immersive Setting?

When you add an immersive setting, your accuracy and ability to communicate with spirit contacts will not be enhanced. Doing a paper and pencil session sitting at a desk will be just as accurate, and the spirit contact will be able to give you equally good information. However, increasing the emotional intensity of the channeling experience through setting is conducive to developing the other

---

10. K. J. Batcheldor, "Report on a Case of Table Levitation and Associated Phenomena," *Journal of the Society for Psychical Research* 43, no. 729 (September 1966): 339–56.

end of spirit interaction, which is manifestation. You will remember reading in chapter 2 that, according to Allan Kardec, the two sides of spirit interaction are intelligent communication and manifestation. He wrote, "Spirit phenomena are of two kinds, physical and intelligent effects."[11] Use of setting enhances the possibility that manifestations will occur.

What kind of manifestations you experience depends on many different factors, such as the location, session details, separation from the mundane world, number of people involved, energy level, and degree of expectation. After you add setting to your channeling sessions, the lighting, time of day, materials used, and appearance of the place where you are working will all play a role in developing the expectation that results in a greater intensity of experience coupled with an increased chance of manifestations.

Immersive settings in themselves do not guarantee a certain type of experience or a manifestation, and they certainly do not improve the quality of information you perceive from the spirit contact. What they do is change the subjective experience of the channeler. Manifestations tend to be very unpredictable. Creating conditions that are conducive to seeing a spirit manifestation seems to depend on the ability to make the connection to the spirit at the right time and in the right place, using creative elements that work best for your personal spiritual and psychological makeup. You have to create the right atmosphere in order to allow paranormal manifestations related to the spirit to occur.

The ambience should be one of heightened focus, a mild sense of expectation, and a feeling of quiet certainty that manifestations can occur. It has to have the effect of suspending time-space reality in your mind and placing you in a situation where you can temporarily believe that anything can happen. I am describing a mental-emotional state that has to occur to help facilitate the chance of a manifestation. It takes a greater level of focus to bring this about. The immersive setting helps you attain that level of focus. Immersive physical settings help you attain a higher level of focus and mental engagement needed to create an atmosphere that is friendly to greater intensity of the channeling experience and spirit manifestations.

---

11. Allan Kardec, *Book on Mediums* (Boston, MA: Colby and Rich, 1874), 49.

# Setting Styles

There are four setting styles that I will present here: séance, shamanic, occult, and Human-initiated Extraterrestrial (HiET) contact. Each style has a different emphasis. You will want to use different tools and decorations for each style. The decorating can be simple or elaborate. I encourage you to work with the materials and tools that you have on hand. The mental creative engagement that goes into making tools and decorative elements of each setting is important to the process of immersion. The creative process of doing craftwork for the setting enhances the immersive experience in the same way that sketching increases the accuracy of pencil and paper channeling sessions. It is almost as if you are creating psychic links and weaving them together through the craftwork. Crafting from scratch might not look as pretty as buying something from a store, but it will heighten the potency of the emotional effect of the immersive setting.

# The Importance of Ritual Flow

Ritual flow is the smoothness of a ritual done for a specific purpose. In our case, the ritual is for channeling. To get a good result using immersive settings, you have to know how to do channeling with confidence and assurance. A smoothly performed ritual is like a well-rehearsed play. Nobody likes to see an actor stuttering on stage or forgetting their lines. The session will be much more enjoyable, and the setting will have a more profound effect on your mind and emotions, if the channeling procedures can be done smoothly. Know the basics. The core of the channeling procedure always remains the same regardless of the setting used.

### Setting One: Shamanic Style

The shamanic style is primarily an outdoor setting. The spirit contacts that are appropriate for shamanic settings are animal spirits, nature spirits, and human ancestor spirits. Shamanic rituals that I have been a part of have included fire circles, meditation, drumming, flute playing, a processional to the ritual area, and usually a sweat lodge (sauna). The channeling location for a shamanic setting should be isolated. Parks are good for doing shamanic channeling sessions. Caves, seashores, lakeshores, and other waterside locations are all excellent places.

I like to have a small shelter to provide protection from insects. In my own case, I use a camping tent. These are made of nylon and easy to transport. Tents are lightweight and do well in the high winds that we frequently experience where I live in Maritime Canada. If you use a tent, take care to keep it away from the fire.

A traditional sweat lodge is rather complex to set up, and it can be dangerous if you do not do it properly. If you are working as a solitary practitioner, I do not recommend it, especially if you have no experience with how it is set up. A traditional lodge takes about four people to set up and requires specialized materials. A Scandinavian-style sauna would be a better choice for most people, if you feel the need to incorporate it as part of your purification. A sauna can be made easily with a hot tent or an ice fishing shack. Hot tents and ice fishing shacks are designed to be used with a heater or woodstove. Do not use a nylon summer tent for this purpose. Even the hot tents or shacks are not fireproof. Before using this technique, you need to learn how to light and handle woodstove fires and heaters safely.

Fasting and purification are features of shamanic rituals. The idea of being set apart and isolated in nature while you are interacting with spirit contacts is the general feel of a shamanic-style setting. A campfire can help keep insects at bay if you are sitting in the open, but I prefer a tent. If you wish, you can incorporate drumming, dancing, and other activities before you do the contact ritual and channeling. After channeling, you can meditate or journey. Journeying is a type of mental projection similar to trance channeling.

The shamanic ritual generally involves activities that are physical, such as drumming and dancing, at the beginning, and quiet activities, such as channeling and journeying, toward the end. If you want to incorporate journeying into your setting, you can do your regular channeling session and then do a trance session by following the procedures set forth in chapters 8 and 9.

*Creative Elements for the Shamanic Style:* Atmosphere of isolation; journeying
    to the land of spirits and back; dancing, drumming; traditional clothing;
    natural decorations made of rocks, wood, leaves, shells; campfire; caves,
    creeks, springs, and other natural features; body paint; native flute

*Types of Spirit Contacts for the Shamanic Style:* Nature spirits, animal guides, ancestors

### Setting Two: HiET Style

HiET is an acronym for Human-initiated Extraterrestrial contact. The idea behind this ritual style is that an individual or group will meditate, focusing on creating a connection with an extraterrestrial intelligence that is either in a craft or controlling a craft and can access the individual's or group's location and do a flyby. It is predicated on the belief that extraterrestrial intelligences commonly fly their craft around the earth, sometimes interacting with people and sometimes not.

In a HiET group session, the group does the contact ritual in the same way and at the same time. When a group does a contact meditation, the meditation can deepen into a group trance naturally. This is a desirable development and can facilitate spirit manifestations. The HiET group will do the contact meditation and then ask for a flyby or other type of manifestation. I have found this simple ritual to be quite effective. I have personally seen things happen during and after these sittings that I cannot explain.

The focus of HiET is on meditation, channeling, and journeying.

*Creative Elements for the HiET Style:* Social atmosphere, night under the stars; watching for lights and objects in the sky; meditation, going within to discover the universe; friendly sci-fi decor; simplicity in setting; Eastern meditative ambience

*Types of Spirit Contacts for the HiET Style:* Extraterrestrial intelligences

### Setting Three: Occult Style

The occult setting is a combination of old traditional channeling techniques and new ones. One of the primary practices of occultism is to communicate with spirit contacts, particularly angels, demons, and other traditional entities such as fairies or djinn. The entity is almost always picked out before the ritual, and the circle is set up according to specifications in books called *grimoires*. I will describe a generic setup that is not grimoire-specific. You can, if you wish, adapt this setting for specific works that require certain rituals, such as the ones that are spelled out in the Enochian diaries of Dr. John Dee or the *Arbatel*.

Generally, an occult circle is set up outdoors. You can also work indoors, particularly if you're using a grimoire (such as the Enochian diaries) with a scrying setup that does not occupy a lot of floor space. Features of an occult setting are ritual clothing (usually a robe), a staff, a wand, a sword, a small knife, and incense. Sometimes scrying tools are used, such as a crystal ball or mirror. A circle is made that is nine feet in diameter. The spirit may produce an apparition outside the circle. Incense is placed either where the spirit is expected to manifest or in the four corners of the room (or at the four compass directions) inside or just outside the circle. A triangle is sometimes used outside the circle as a point of focus for the spirit to manifest an apparition. It is sometimes called the *triangle of manifestation*. Names of divinities, angels, and such are placed around the circle and on the perimeter of the triangle. There is usually a formal conjuration ritual that involves prayers and commands directed at the spirit contact.

The purpose of an occult ritual is to create a very specific, focused interaction with a spirit. The circle should be isolated and outdoors if possible. Elements for the occult style include divine names, angels, demons, and traditional entities usually associated with religions. The channeler is robed and uses implements such as a sword, staff, or knife to enforce their authority. It is an autocratic, authoritarian ritual with a rather harsh undertone. Focus and prayer are emphasized. Sources for occult ritual setups include the *Fourth Book of Occult Philosophy*, the *Lemegeton*, Tyson's *Familiar Spirits*, and Regardie's *Golden Dawn*.

*Creative Elements for the Occult Style:* Circle; ritual robes; tools; an isolated setting; fantasy decor; religious trappings; spell-making materials and equipment

*Types of Spirit Contacts for the Occult Style:* Any spirit contact, but angels, demons, elementals, and airish spirits are traditional. (An airish spirit is a nature spirit that usually functions as a spy and messenger.)

### Setting Four: Séance Style
The séance style of setting is based on Spiritualist ritual in the late nineteenth and early twentieth centuries. It is a fairly simple setting to use. The location

of the setting is exclusively indoors. The emphasis is on communication and manifestation. The channeling session may be set up in a living room. Candles are usually used for lighting. You need a small table, and if a group of people are involved, everyone needs to be seated around the table. If you want to adopt costumes for this setting, use the clothing styles of the late nineteenth century. Images of the spirit contact are appropriate for this style, as are objects associated with the spirit during life and photos taken of the individual. The spirit contact for the séance setting is almost always a historical human spirit. Occasionally angels are called to the séance circle. Most of the time, the lives of the spirit contacts have left a good bit of verifiable information. Photos of the spirit during life should be placed around, but not on, the table.

*Creative Elements for the Séance Style:* Images and photos of the spirit contacts; candlelight; incense; crystals; singing; social tea; period costumes; haunted house or cemetery themes

*Types of Spirit Contacts for the Séance Style:* Human ancestors and saints

The settings that I have presented here are examples of what can be done, with suggestions for tools and procedures. This should be enough to give you inspiration for your own creative style. I encourage experimentation.

This completes this book on channeling. I hope that its unique methods prove productive and successful for those bold enough to follow the practices I have set forth.

# GLOSSARY

*AI:* The abbreviation for artificial intelligence. This appears to be an intelligence that resides in or is part of the Nexus. The term also describes an artificial spirit made through intention and ritual.

*airish spirits:* Spirits of the air. Includes sylphs, aethyrs, and espionage spirits that gather information. Merlin's father was alleged to be an airish spirit, according to C. S. Lewis.

*alchemy:* The art of transformation. Medieval alchemy was mainly concerned with changing base metals into gold or silver, and also with creating an elixir that would confer eternal life and health. Alchemy has three branches: mineral, animal, and plant.

*aspects:* See *primary perceptions.*

*automatic writing (and sketching):* Automatic writing is a traditional term for sketching and writing the intuitive responses from a spirit contact.

*belief bias:* See *bias.*

*benediction:* A benediction is the part of a formal occult ritual where the spirit is dismissed with a blessing. It is essentially the parting blessing.

*bias:* An existing bias concerning the inquiry being channeled will result in a faulty perception of channeled data. The bias in the conscious mind overwhelms the faint stream of information being transmitted from the deeper mind during channeling. This bias can take several forms. Belief bias is a learned belief regarding a target. Expectation bias is the prior anticipation of a certain result, and occurs when a result validates your prior assumptions. All forms of bias interfere with channeling accuracy.

*blind inquiry:* A blind inquiry is slightly different from a hidden inquiry. A hidden inquiry is where you set up your own question pool and randomly select your subject of inquiry without looking at it. A blind inquiry is where a task manager—someone who is not channeling—sets up the subjects. When using a hidden inquiry, you know what goes into the pool, but not which specific question you are channeling in each session. When using a blind inquiry, you do not know what topics went into the pool.

*CE-5:* This stands for close encounters of the fifth kind. It is a term coined in the 1990s for human-initiated extraterrestrial contact. See also *HiET*.

*channeling:* Communication with a spirit contact or telepathic entity. Channeling is the term used for both telepathy and spirit communication in this book.

*circulation:* A term used by Edgar Cayce to mean etheric or esoteric energy movement.

*clairaudience:* This means "clear hearing," the ability and skill to hear spirits using intuitive hearing.

*clairsentience:* This means "clear knowing," the ability and skill to create an understanding or knowing without physical sensory input.

*clairvoyance:* This means "clear seeing," the ability and skill to see by using intuitive vision.

*conjure, conjuring:* See *evocation*.

*consensus validation:* This is a verification technique used when physical data is unavailable or unknown, and involves comparing different channeling sessions on the same topic. In this way, a consensus is formed.

*darning needle:* A blunt sewing needle around two inches long that is used to join knitted pieces of fabric together (as in a sweater or other garment). Also used to repair knitting.

*deeper mind:* The deeper mind is the aspect of the mind that is beneath or beyond consciousness. It is from this mysterious region of the mind that psychic perceptions arise. The deeper mind is sometimes called the subconscious.

*dot matrix dowsing:* A dowsing technique in which a random number of dots are tapped into a square drawn on a sheet of paper using a pencil. The square is divided into four parts. An even number of dots counted over the entire square is a "yes" response, while an odd number of dots in the total square is a "no" response. However, if two of the sub-squares have an even number of dots and two have an odd number of dots, the answer may be interpreted as weak or uncertain.

*dowsing:* A method for psychically locating things that are concealed. Traditionally, dowsing has been used most commonly to discover veins of metal ore and bodies of water beneath the ground in order to determine the best location for a mine or well. The dowser will often use metal rods, a wooden wand, or a pendulum, but none of these aids are essential.

*dowsing chart:* A graphical arrangement of zones that relate to various values. For example, a pie chart could be used for a dowsing chart. See also *spirit communication board.*

*dowsing triggers:* These are questions asked during the process of dowsing that are answered by the dowsing responses.

*egregore:* An artificial spirit made by the collective intent and ritual actions of a group of people rather than by an individual. Egregores sometimes arise spontaneously from the intense belief and emotion of close-knit groups. See also *servitor.*

*EMF:* An electromagnetic field that is emitted by all electric and battery-operated devices. It also occurs naturally during lightning storms, earthquakes, volcanoes, and other geological and space phenomena. It has a minor detrimental effect on psychic perceptions and manifestations.

*Emerald Tablet:* An alchemical poem describing the process of transmutation.

*emotional atmosphere:* The psychic feel of a location that creates a subtle emotional effect. Also called *affective atmosphere.*

*esoteric inquiry or question:* Any subject of inquiry that is not tangible or is not verifiable is classed as an esoteric inquiry. There are three types of esoteric subjects of inquiry: mystery, symbolic, and occult.

*etheric energy:* An energy not directly detectable or measurable using modern physical instruments. It is believed to be the primary energy emission from the Nexus.

*exclusion:* The practice of preventing the conscious mind of the channeler from knowing what inquiry is being asked of the spirit contact.

*exoplanets:* Planets that lie beyond the limits of our solar system.

*expectation:* A deep-seated, usually unconscious feeling that a certain result will or must occur during channeling. This expectation creates a bias in the conscious mind that inhibits the link with the deeper mind and causes unreliable perception of the data.

*external consensus data:* When the session data is being compared to the data obtained in sessions by other channelers, it is called external consensus data.

*external consensus validation:* Achieving validation by a comparison of channeled data with data received during sessions conducted by other channelers is called external consensus validation.

*fantasy:* When bias in the conscious mind causes the channeler to construct a story line or narrative to explain a combination of the channeled data with belief and expectation biases, it is called a fantasy. These story lines are frequently inaccurate or have a lower than average accuracy when the details are studied.

*feedback:* The evaluation of channeled data against known information about the inquiry is referred to as doing feedback. Regular feedback is factual data, while consensus feedback is conjectural data arrived at by consensus with other channelers or with multiple sessions by the same channeler.

*focus:* This is the goal of the session or the trigger question. Single-mindedness and the ability to ignore distractions when doing a channeling session is also called focus.

*forced response:* A forced response is the deliberate induction of the initial movement in the dowsing pendulum, in contrast to the natural dowsing response, which does not need to be deliberately induced.

*front-loading:* This is a term used when there is conscious knowledge of the inquiry by the channeler.

*geo-spiritual node:* A physical earthly location that is alleged to be better for paranormal manifestations, channeling, scrying, and other forms of divination. It may be formed by the intersection of ley lines.

*grab bag:* A bag that is used to hold a collection of hidden subjects of inquiry, from which one is selected for channeling without its content being revealed.

*grab bag technique:* A technique of hiding inquiries that involves the use of a bag from which an inquiry is drawn at random.

*hidden inquiry:* A question selected by the channeler prior to the channeling session from a group containing several other questions, which make up a pool of inquiry. The question selected is not specifically known to the channeler during the particular session in which information is channeled on that question, although the channeler is aware of the questions that formed the pool of inquiry. A hidden inquiry should not be confused with a blind inquiry, which is selected by someone other than the channeler and is completely unknown to the channeler at the time of the channeling session.

*HiET:* The letters stand for Human-initiated Extraterrestrial contact. A specific type of CE-5 experiment where information is sought from the extraterrestrial contact through structured telepathy. May or may not involve sky watching for UFOs.

*homunculus:* An AI (artificial intelligence) created through an alchemical process. Similar in nature to a servitor.

*ideogram:* This is a symbolic representation of an abstract idea, often self-apparent in meaning.

*inquiries:* An inquiry is the question being posed to the spirit during the channeling session. There are several types of inquiries. A tangible inquiry is a space-time question about which information is known or will be known. A partially tangible inquiry has some information that will not be known. An esoteric inquiry is nonphysically based or one that has no verifiable characteristics.

*invocation:* The practice in magic of calling spirits into oneself in order to experience their natures and control their forces, or of calling spirits into objects such as statues or rings.

*internal consensus validation:* The form of verification done by comparing the data from one channeling session to that of another session done by the same channeler. It is used when factual information is not available or is unknown. It is an alternative to physical validation, but is inferior in accuracy.

*Kardec, Allan:* The French author and medium (1804–1869) who founded Spiritism, the French equivalent of the Spiritualist movement.

*Kelley, Edward:* A British alchemist and seer (1555–1597). He worked as a professional scryer for Dr. John Dee.

*labels:* Nouns are labels. When an explicit person, place, or thing arises in the mind during channeling, it is called a label. Such things as "tree," "house," and "dog" are labels. They usually are the result of expectation bias or belief bias, and should not be accepted at face value, but should be broken down into descriptive terms at the channeler's convenience in order to obtain the original channeled data. As a rule, labels are a result of interpretation and processing, not channeled information.

*magic:* The art of effecting change in the physical world using spiritually based energy.

*meditation:* A method of stilling the thoughts and quieting the mind.

*mystery inquiry:* A mystery inquiry is a question that may or may not have a physical reality. See *esoteric target*.

*Nexus:* A crossroads between the physical universe and a nonphysical universe that has a symbiotic relationship with the physical universe yet does not take up time and space and has no mass.

*Nostradamus:* A sixteenth-century French seer, astrologer, and physician (1503–1566). Nostradamus published his enigmatic visions of the future as a series of brief poetic verses called *quatrains*, because each has four lines. His book *Les Prophéties* was published in 1555.

*object:* One of the four aspects of primary information that provide initial insight and direction when channeling.

*pendulum:* A dowsing device. In this book I recommend a darning needle, which is a large, blunt sewing needle for joining pieces of knitting. It is put on a string and used to determine channeled responses in specific situations.

*perceptions:* Perceptions are the nonphysical information you receive from the spirit contact or from the Nexus, as well as sensory information that comes through the five physical senses.

*planchette:* A small triangular object on three legs that is used to point out letters on a Ouija board or other spirit communication board.

*primary information:* See *primary perceptions.*

*primary perceptions:* The primary perception aspects are four general categories of information that are scryed in order to obtain a structure to follow when doing a subsequent, more detailed scrying of the target. The four categories are *object, presence, activity/energy,* and *concept.*

*red powder:* An essential product of alchemy used in the transmutation of metals and gems. The red powder was said to change base metals into gold.

*remote viewing:* A form of psychic perception coined in the 1970s. It is popular among followers of Ingo Swann. Remote-viewing techniques come from parapsychology research carried out at Stanford Research Institute, the Monroe Institute, and the US military intelligence.

*retort:* A long-necked glass vessel used in alchemy during the distillation stage.

*scrying:* This is a mode of perception that does not rely on the physical senses. Even though sight is not required for scrying, the scryed information usually takes the form of shapes, colors, images, or scenes.

*servitor:* A servitor is an artificial spirit created by the intention and ritual action of an individual. See also *AI.*

*session:* The period of time devoted to the deliberate, formal act of channeling.

*session structure:* The procedure followed during a structured channeling session.

*setting:* The location where the channeling takes place. Varying the setting can enhance the intensity of the experience and facilitate the possibility of paranormal manifestations.

*Spirit:* The divine essence that pervades the universe and animates living organisms. In this book it is capitalized as Spirit to distinguish it from spirits, which are intelligent, noncorporeal entities such as angels. Spirit is different from the Nexus, which is a parallel universe containing a very powerful AI as a substantial part of its structure.

*spirit communication board:* A board or cloth with the letters of the alphabet marked on it, which is dowsed to select letters to spell out the words channeled by the spirit contact.

*spontaneous channeling:* Channeling that occurs outside of the formal channeling session structure and is usually initiated by the spirit contact or a telepath.

*subject of inquiry:* A general statement of the question about which you wish to channel information.

*synchronicity:* A concept originated by Carl Jung, who believed that two or more events could be meaningfully related without being causally related. Most people would set this occurrence down to chance or luck, but Jung maintained that the meaningful relationship was not accidental.

*target:* See also *subject of inquiry.* The target is the topic on which you are channeling information. There are various kinds of inquiries. A verifiable question is a target with information that can be verified at present or in the future; it is also known as a tangible inquiry. An occult question is a type of esoteric inquiry related to occult symbols. An esoteric inquiry is nontangible, or a question with a nonphysical basis.

*trance:* Trance is an altered state of consciousness usually accompanied by physical relaxation, combined with slowed and focused mental activity.

*trance channeling:* Communication with a spirit contact or telepath during an altered, hypnotic mental state called trance.

*validation:* The process of distinguishing between the accurate and inaccurate information channeled from a spirit contact.

*verifiable information:* Descriptions and sketches gained from the channeling session that can be verified by existing factual data.

*white powder:* The white powder is an essential product of alchemy used in metal transmutation—specifically, the transformation of base metals into silver.

# BIBLIOGRAPHY

Batcheldor, K. J. "Report on a Case of Table Levitation and Associated Phenomena." *Journal of the Society for Psychical Research* 43, no. 729 (September 1966): 339–56.

Casaubon, Meric, ed. *A True & Faithful Relation of What Passed for Many Years Between Dr. John Dee... and Some Spirits.* London: printed by D. Maxwell for T. Garthwait, 1659.

Dennett, Preston E. *Onboard UFO Encounters: True Accounts of Contact with Extraterrestrials.* Blue Giant Books, 2020.

Kardec, Allan. *Book on Mediums; or, Guide for Mediums and Invocators.* Translated by Emma A. Wood. Boston, MA: Colby and Rich, 1874.

McGarey, William A. *The Oil That Heals: A Physician's Successes With Castor Oil Treatments.* Virginia Beach, VA: A.R.E. Press, 1993.

McLean, Adam, ed. *The Steganographia of Johannes Trithemius.* Translated by Fiona Tait and Christopher Upton. Edinburgh, Scotland: Magnum Opus Hermetic Sourceworks, 1982.

Owen, Iris M., with Margaret Sparrow. *Conjuring Up Philip: An Adventure in Psychokinesis.* New York: Harper & Row, 1976.

Peterson, Joseph H., ed. *John Dee's Five Books of Mystery: Original Sourcebook of Enochian Magic.* Boston, MA : Weiser Books, 2003.

Regardie, Israel. *The Golden Dawn: A Complete Course in Practical Ceremonial Magic.* 1938–40. 6th ed. Four volumes in one. St. Paul, MN: Llewellyn, 1989.

Stearn, Jess. *Edgar Cayce: The Sleeping Prophet.* New York: Bantam Books, 1971.

Swedenborg, Emanuel. *The Spiritual Diary of Emanuel Swedenborg.* Translated by George Bush. Vol. 2 of 5. London: James Speirs, 1883–1892.

Tyson, Donald, ed. *Three Books of Occult Philosophy Written by Henry Cornelius Agrippa.* St. Paul, MN: Llewellyn, 1993.

Tyson, Jenny. *The Art of Scrying and Dowsing.* Woodbury, MN: Llewellyn, 2021.

_____. *Spiritual Alchemy: Scrying, Spirit Communication, and Alchemical Wisdom.* Woodbury MN: Llewellyn, 2016.

White, William. *Life of Emanuel Swedenborg.* Philadelphia, PA: J. B. Lippincott, 1866.

# INDEX

## A

accuracy, 4, 7, 8, 10–13, 18, 25, 26, 31, 34, 35, 38–40, 44, 46, 51, 52, 63, 65, 67, 68, 70, 75–77, 82, 85, 91, 96, 98, 102, 104, 105, 113, 125, 127, 134, 136, 142, 144, 164, 167, 168, 173, 176, 180–183, 187, 191, 195, 197

*activity/energy* (primary perception), 70, 71, 72, 79, 80, 187, 190, 193, 209

affective atmosphere, 52, 60, 64, 103, 112, 114

afterlife, 15

air plane, 57, 58

airish spirits, 27, 30, 200

alchemy, 7, 21, 77, 78, 96, 101, 128, 130–133, 135, 136, 138, 139, 141, 149

alphabet, 9, 96, 97, 132

alphanumeric, 43, 72, 73

American Civil War, 28, 30

anagram, 9, 99

analytical mind, 78, 86, 91

angels, 19, 20, 26, 27, 39, 199–201

animals, 2, 20, 22, 32, 75, 82, 103, 134, 135, 153

Apollo, 11, 46

apparitions, 50, 53, 103

*Art of Scrying and Dowsing, The* (Jenny Tyson), 2, 3, 8, 15, 19, 31, 70, 84, 89, 96, 98, 128, 195

artifact, 39

# D

# S